# cooking easier, healthier & better

## 150+ DELICIOUS RECIPES

### New Steamer Function with Easy and Fast Steamer Recipes

### 2nd EDITION

**RULE THE KITCHEN**

*4-in-1*

COOKING SYSTEM

Nutritional Analyses: Calculations for the nutritional analyses in this book are based on the largest number of servings listed within the recipes. Calculations are rounded up to the nearest gram or milligram, as appropriate. If two options for an ingredient are listed, the first one is used. Not included are optional ingredients or serving suggestions.

Editors: Mona Wetter Dolgov and Bob Warden • Graphic Designer: Leslie Anne Feagley
Photo Creative Director: Anne Sommers Welch • Photography: Quentin Bacon • Additional Photography: Gary Sloan and Heath Robbins • Food Stylist: Mariana Velasquez • Recipe Development: Euro-Pro Test Kitchen Team and Culinary Palette, Bob Warden, Carole Haffey, Amy Golino, Kimberly Letizia, and Vanessa Spillios

Published in the United States of America by
Great Flavors LLC
New Hope, PA 18938
www.greatchefsinternational.com

ISBN: 978-1-4951-1017-7

Printed in China

# TABLE OF CONTENTS

# YOUR NINJA 4-IN-1 COOKING SYSTEM: COOKING EASIER, EATING BETTER

One thing almost everybody has in common today: There are tons of things to manage and the clock is always ticking. Wherever we go, whatever we do, it seems like we never have enough time to do the things we want to do. Whether you are a seasoned home chef or a novice in the kitchen trying to get a quick meal on the table, your Ninja 4-in-1 Cooking System will help you make your meals more flavorful and healthier, with ease, speed, and true convenience.

The Ninja 4-in-1 Cooking System with Triple Fusion Heat Technology does it all. Your advanced system combines oven, stovetop cooking, slow cooking, conventional steaming, steam roasting, and baking technology to enhance flavors, making meats juicier, meals healthier, and desserts more moist, and elevating your family meals from ordinary to extraordinary. It puts success on your table with these versatile features:

**FAST ONE-POT MEAL MAKING** — Now, with your Ninja Cooking System's Triple Fusion Heat, you can make complete meals for your family in just one single pot. You can layer meals and cook pasta, veggies, and meats all at the same time — pasta does not even have to be drained! Casseroles come out extra crispy on both the bottom and sides. You can even prepare delicious meals from frozen and take them right to your table in 30 minutes or less. Use either the STOVETOP or Triple Fusion Heat OVEN setting!

**STEAM OVEN ROASTING** — How do you bring out the best quality in practically any cut of meat? Sear first by using STOVETOP HIGH, place meat on rack, and then simply add water to the pot to create a steam infusion. Set to your desired temperature, and begin steam roasting! Steam-infused roasting cuts the cooking time by up to 30 percent and makes your meats juicier. By adding herbs, broth, or wine to your water, you'll add extra-delicious flavors. Try our recommended flavor infusions from our provided chart for added inspiration.

**STEAMER** — The Ninja 4-in-1 Cooking System can also be used to automatically steam vegetables, fish, and meat in less time than most dedicated steamers. When set to the STEAMER function, the system has the power to continually produce a high volume of steam. The heavy glass lid helps create a steam environment of approximately 224° F. Now you can easily steam your favorite vegetables, fish, and poultry. The surround-steam environment will allow faster steam times. Our handy steamer chart on page 236 and built-in timer will guide you to delicious, foolproof cooking with perfect cooking results.

**STEAM OVEN BAKING** — Baking this modern way might be new to you, but it's another feature that makes the Ninja 4-in-1 Cooking System a truly breakthrough appliance. Leave your oven off. You'll find that steam baking delivers lighter, richer puddings and moist, higher-rising cakes. Plus, you only have to use half the fat! This means healthier, lower-calorie desserts — even at less than 50 calories — using this new revolutionary style to bake!

**SEARIOUS/SLOW COOKING** — To make more flavorful meals, professional chefs sear meats and sauté vegetables before slow cooking. Until now, that meant an extra step of heating up a second skillet pan, and at least one more pan to wash. The Ninja 4-in-1 Cooking System lets you sear, brown, and slow cook meats right in the same appliance, with its built-in stovetop. Plus, the slow cooker is programmable, allowing you to set the cooking time, and it will automatically keep warm once cooking is complete. It's a convenient way to cook, making meal preparation and cleanup easier.

# USING THE NINJA 4-IN-1 COOKING SYSTEM COOKBOOK

This cookbook provides recipes and tips you'll find invaluable. They'll help you use the Ninja 4-in-1 Cooking System to simplify your preparation for all of your meals.

Take a minute to look them over. We've included 150 recipes, each customized for the Ninja 4-in-1 Cooking System, that have all been developed and tested in our Ninja kitchens. The recipes tell you exactly what you need for the dish and how to prepare it — clear directions for reliable success. At the top of each recipe, we explain benefits and best uses. You'll also find at least one tip for healthy ingredient choices, time-saving methods, or serving suggestions.

Nine chapters share the secrets of using the Ninja 4-in-1 Cooking System for exciting results:

**30-MINUTE MEALS:** Easy meals perfect for a weeknight — fast, satisfying, complete.

LITE FARE (HEALTHY & DELICIOUS): Healthier meals, with an eye on lower calories and fat.

**APPETIZERS:** Formal starters or yummy party snacks for entertaining.

**SOUPS/STEWS:** Hearty and savory, even perfect for a lighter meal!

**STEAMED DISHES:** Healthy, delicious, and simple techniques to prepare foods in less than 15 minutes!

ENTRÉES: Main courses your family — and even guests — will love.

SIDE DISHES: Speedy, delicious accompaniments all made in one pot!

**DESSERTS:** Tempting treats made healthier without the need of your home stove.

**BREAKFASTS:** Surprise! Make the first meal of the day easy and delicious!

Time to get started! Pick a recipe from any chapter and give it a try. We built the Ninja 4-in-1 Cooking System to make your life easier. It's one kitchen appliance that eliminates problems and guesswork. Use it every day to save time while preparing meals you're proud to serve.

Have fun!
*The NINJA Kitchen Team*

# ⊚ Stovetop

SEAR & SAUTÉ — It's a trick that savvy cooks have known for years — searing and browning meat and sautéing vegetables develops added flavors, color, and texture to your meals. The result: tender, juicier, more flavorful meats and sweeter aromatic vegetables. Searing meats especially adds attractive color, crusty texture, and flavor contrast you expect from the best restaurant meals. You can now bring that same quality to your home-cooked meals simply and easily, all in one pot.

For the first time, the Ninja 4-in-1 Cooking System lets you sear, brown, or sauté using the STOVETOP setting. It's quick and simple. Just put the ingredients in the pot, set the STOVETOP to the correct setting, and go!

This STOVETOP feature is versatile, too. The LOW setting simmers soups and sauces, and HIGH browns meats and tender vegetables. Also use the HIGH to prepare a complete skillet or stir-fry dinner and to reheat dinners, too!

Use the STOVETOP setting for sequential cooking — that means, sear meats on STOVETOP HIGH before you slow cook or steam roast to prepare the most delicious meals. This setting will allow your ingredients to lock in the flavor!

## Tips & Tricks

1. **The preset temperatures are similar to your stovetop on LOW, or HIGH.**

2. **Do not use the lid when using the STOVETOP HIGH setting to prevent burning of food.**

3. **Use the STOVETOP HIGH setting to make gravies from your liquids after you roast — all in the same pot!**

4. **For healthier cooking, remove any excess fat from the cooking pot before roasting. Be sure to wear protective mitts when handling unit.**

5. **For quicker browning, set to STOVETOP HIGH for 2–3 minutes before placing ingredients in pot.**

# Fast One-Pot Meal Making

**ONE-POT MEALS —** Your Ninja 4-in-1 Cooking System's Triple Fusion Heat Technology provides heat to both the sides and bottom of the pot that allows you to create complete meals all at the same time — from Chicken Piccata to Spaghetti and Meatballs! This means no extra pans for browning foods or preparing more complex dishes. Now, when your meals are complete, you will have only one pot to clean. You can even prepare meals with pasta in the same pot — by layering the foods in the right way, pasta will be ready, without the need to drain!

**LAYERED MEALS —** For the first time, you can prepare complete meals in a single pot. Even challenging dishes like layered casseroles cook up beautifully with every ingredient done properly — vegetables, crispy toppings, and meats prepared to family-pleasing perfection. The rack included can accommodate the different meal components. Typically, place your starch on the bottom with the appropriate broth or water and place your protein and vegetables on the rack during cooking. The rack makes it easy to check for doneness and to remove each meal component when it is perfectly cooked.

Achieve impressive food quality with one-pot convenience!

## Tips & Tricks

1. **Dense root vegetables cook slower than many meat cuts or more tender veggies. Cut them into small uniform pieces so they'll cook at the same rate as other ingredients.**

2. **Vegetables can be added with starches in layered meals to add more flavorful dishes.**

3. **Frozen fish and chicken breasts cook perfectly on the rack or right in the pot, and you can prepare meals in less than 30 minutes.**

4. **See our charts in the back of the book for cooking guides for meats, vegetables, and starches for inspiration and to manage getting your meals complete at the same time.**

**EASY SPAGHETTI & MEATBALLS**

#  SEARious Slow Cooking

**SLOW COOKING** — The Ninja 4-in-1 Cooking System is also a SEARious slow cooker — the STOVETOP setting allows you to sear your meats first, then SLOW COOK all in the same appliance! Searing not only gives great texture, it also builds flavor profiles that will elevate your dishes to gourmet quality. The SLOW COOK feature allows you to cook food all day, and it is safe to leave home while cooking! Cook on LOW for all-day cooking or cook on HIGH in half the time, great for weekend comfort-food cooking. Whether cooking savory Hearty Beef Stew, Pulled Pork & Apple Cider Sliders, or a White Turkey Chili, this portable counter top appliance offers versatile convenience when cooking new and old favorite recipes to treat your family and friends all year long. In addition, use your SEARious slow cooker to make healthier and lighter vegetable dishes, too! See all of our delicious recipes!

## Tips & Tricks

1. **Never fill your pot more than ⅔ full to ensure food is cooked appropriately.**

2. **Lifting the lid during cooking may increase the total cook time.**

3. **Because our slow cooking uses very little energy, it is great to slow cook in the hot summer months to keep your kitchen cool.**

4. **While some frozen foods can be cooked successfully in the slow-cooker mode, it may increase the total cook time. Always use an instant-read thermometer to ensure that foods are cooked to the correct internal temperature. Large frozen roasts are not recommended to be slow cooked. To ensure proper cook time and doneness, it is best to thaw meat safely in the refrigerator before cooking.**

5. **Certain dried spices can even intensify during slow cooking such as chili pepper powders, cayenne, and red pepper flakes. Use half of the amount of hot spice at the beginning, and add more at the end if necessary.**

6. **Pouring off or skimming fat that has rendered off during searing or slow cooking will reduce the overall fat content of your dishes to make them healthier for your family.**

7. **Use the programmability — set the cooking time, and the unit will automatically shift to AUTO WARM until you are ready to enjoy!**

PORK CHOPS PROVENÇAL

# 🔲 Steam Oven

**STEAM ROASTING** — The Ninja 4-in-1 Cooking System has steam-oven capability to make your meats juicier and reduce cooking time by up to 30 percent! The combination of radiant and steam heat makes preparation of poultry, beef, pork, and even fish simple, easy, and delicious. Taking less time and cooking in a steam environment results in juicy, flavorful roasts. You will taste the difference right away ... tender, flavorful perfection.

It's easy to steam roast! Simply add water or flavorful infusion into the pot. Place the rack with your seasoned meat into the pot, set the oven to your desired temperature setting, set the cook time, and start roasting. You will not only save cooking time, but there is also NO PREHEATING REQUIRED!

We've described a series of flavor infusions that actually bring rich taste into the food while it cooks. Check out our flavor-infusion charts in the back of the book for delicious ideas!

## Tips & Tricks

1. **Spray the rack with nonstick cooking spray before you cook. Meats won't stick, and cleanup will be even easier.**

2. **Arranging foods in even layers on the rack promotes even cooking.**

3. **Wait 5–10 minutes after roasting meat before you serve, to let the meat rest and the juices settle. The juices distribute evenly, and everything tastes even better.**

4. **Keep the rack level when you lift it out so food won't slide or roll off.**

5. **Protect yourself — always use oven mitts or pot holders when you remove the rack.**

6. **Try roasting with or without the rack. Many cooks make a "rack" of root or aromatic vegetables (like shallots, onion chunks, or potatoes) to support the meat. This adds flavor in both directions.**

SWEET & SPICY PORK BABY BACK RIBS

# Steamer

**STEAMER —** Steam cooking is easy and fast when you use the STEAMER function for your favorite vegetables and light entrees. Refer to the steam chart found on page 236. Fill the pot with the recommended amount of water. Set to STEAMER, then set the timer, using the recommended times. While the water comes to a boil, prepare your food for steaming, and place on metal rack. After the beep (about 7-10 minutes), carefully place the rack with the food in the Ninja 4-in-1 Cooking System. Place the lid on the pot. The timer will automatically count down to your desired cooking time and beep when cooking is complete. Need more time? Simply add more time using the dial.

## Tips & Tricks

1. Most vegetables will cook in just a few minutes, and 2 cups of water is usually sufficient. If cooking time takes more than 10 minutes, check the water level occasionally and if necessary add more water from a boiling kettle.

2. Make sure vegetables are not tightly packed on the rack. It is important that the steam can move through and around vegetable pieces to insure even cooking.

3. To check doneness safely, turn off the cooker, lift the lid away from you, and let the steam escape. Then use long tongs or a protective mitt to avoid exposing your hands to the pot interior. Steam can cause a serious burn in an instant.

4. Avoid overcooking of vegetables by quickly cooling them with water right after steaming. For added flavor, you can toss the vegetables with a light coating of olive oil.

5. If you are cooking vegetables ahead, rinse in cold water immediately after steaming to stop cooking. Drain well and store refrigerated in a tightly sealed zip-top bag or airtight storage container.

6. You can steam frozen vegetables, but you should rinse them in cold water before cooking. Place them in a colander and make sure all vegetables are separated with no clumping.

7. Steaming is best for thinner cuts of fish fillets, boneless chicken breasts, and shellfish.

ITALIAN GREEN BEANS

# Steam Baking

**STEAM BAKING** — The Ninja 4-in-1 Cooking System also steam bakes to make your desserts moister and healthier. By baking in a steam environment, you only have to use HALF the fat, plus you get cakes that are spongier and more delicious. This results in healthier desserts that taste yummy! Prepare tasty cupcakes and loaf cakes — cheesecakes and pudding cakes also taste lighter and more delectable! It's an easy way to indulge and save calories!

It is really simple to steam bake in the Ninja 4-in-1 Cooking System. Place water at the bottom of the pot. Place your baking pan with batter on the rack, set to OVEN, set your desired temperature and time, and start baking!

## Tips & Tricks

1. The pot's nonstick coating makes a great baking surface. You'll only need a nonstick spray if the recipe calls for it.

2. Always use oven mitts or pot holders when you remove the rack from the pot.

3. A handy rule of thumb for steam baking: Add a cup of water for about every 10 minutes of baking time.

4. Fruited-topping cakes are made best when the fruit is placed on the bottom of the pan. Lift the cake out of the pan to create delicious fruited upside-down cakes.

MINI CHEESECAKES

**COD WITH TOMATO CAPER SAUCE & SUGAR SNAP PEAS**

# CHAPTER 1: 30-Minute Meals

⊚ ▤ S T O V E T O P / O V E N

*Signature*

# HEARTY SKILLET LASAGNA

Easiest lasagna ever! Brown meat and cook noodles, then finish it off with spinach and cheeses — all in the same pot! Covered cooking makes this recipe almost foolproof, so you can experiment and try different sauces, greens, and cheeses.

**PREP:** 5 minutes • **COOK:** 25 minutes • **SERVINGS:** 6

## Ingredients

**1 pound lean ground beef**

**10 uncooked lasagna noodles, broken into 2-inch pieces**

**1 jar (24 ounces) pasta sauce**

**1½ cups water**

**1 package (about 6 ounces) fresh baby spinach**

**1 cup shredded mozzarella cheese**

**½ cup ricotta cheese**

**¼ cup shredded Parmesan cheese**

## Directions

**1.** Place beef into pot. Set to STOVETOP HIGH. Cook uncovered 10 minutes or until beef is browned, stirring often.

**2.** Arrange noodle pieces over beef. Pour sauce and water over noodles. Set to OVEN at 350°F. Cover and cook 15–20 minutes or until noodles are tender. Turn off pot.

**3.** Stir in spinach. Stir cheeses in bowl. Spoon cheese mixture over noodle mixture. Cover and let stand.

**NINJA** HEALTHY TIP

Replace ground beef with ground turkey or chicken and add 1 tablespoon olive oil to pot before browning. Also, substitute part-skim mozzarella cheese and low-fat or even fat-free ricotta for those listed in the recipe.

 OVEN

# EASY SPAGHETTI & MEATBALLS

The perfect combination of ingredients means that pasta, meatballs, and sauce can cook together in the pot — no prep needed! This family favorite is a true one-dish meal.

**PREP:** 5 minutes  •  **COOK:** 25 minutes  •  **SERVINGS:** 4

## Ingredients

**4 cups water**

**1 pound spaghetti, broken in half**

**1 jar (24 ounces) pasta sauce (for thinner sauce, reduce water by ¼ cup)**

**1 package (24 ounces) frozen meatballs**

## Directions

1. Pour water into pot. Stir in spaghetti, sauce, and meatballs. Set OVEN to 300°F for 25 minutes. Cover and cook until pasta is tender and meatballs are hot, stirring occasionally.
NOTE: When using thinner sauces, use 3¾ cups water. For whole-grain and thicker pastas, increase cooking time by 2–5 minutes, or until pasta is tender. Serve immediately.

 **NINJA** SERVING TIP

Serve with a tossed green salad and garlic bread.

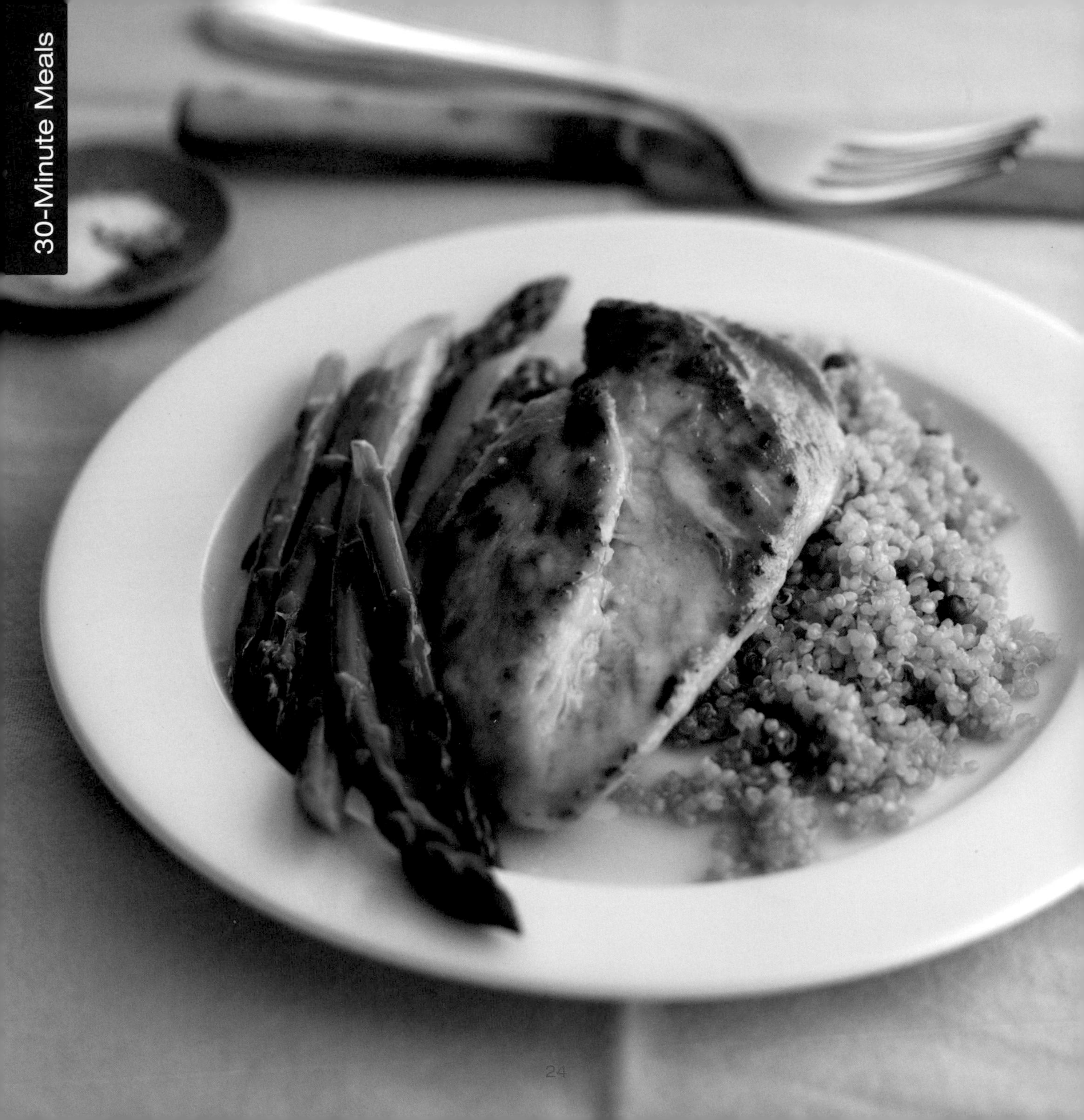

 STOVETOP/STEAM OVEN

# CHICKEN PICCATA

Sautéed chicken breasts, quinoa cooked with lemon and wine, and perfectly steamed asparagus, cooked in 30 minutes using only one pot! Layered cooking makes it easy to serve a homemade meal in minutes.

**PREP:** 5 minutes  •  **COOK:** 25 minutes  •  **SERVINGS:** 4

## Ingredients

**2 tablespoons all-purpose flour**

**¼ teaspoon salt**

**⅛ teaspoon ground black pepper**

**1¼ pounds boneless, skinless, thin-sliced chicken breast halves**

**2 tablespoons olive oil**

**2 tablespoons butter**

**1 cup chicken broth**

**1 cup dry white wine**

**⅓ cup lemon juice**

**¼ cup brined capers, rinsed and drained**

**1 cup uncooked quinoa, rinsed**

**1¼ pounds fresh asparagus, cut into ½-inch pieces**

**parsley for garnish**

## Directions

**1.** Stir flour, salt, and black pepper on plate. Coat chicken with flour mixture.

**2.** Add oil and butter to pot. Set to STOVETOP HIGH and heat until butter is melted. Add chicken to pot. Cook uncovered 10 minutes or until chicken is lightly browned on both sides. Remove chicken from pot and place on rack.

**3.** Add broth, wine, lemon juice, and capers to pot. Stir in quinoa. Place rack with chicken in pot, and place asparagus on rack with chicken. Set OVEN to 300°F for 15 minutes. Cover until chicken is cooked through, asparagus is tender, and quinoa breaks apart.

**4.** Remove asparagus and chicken from pot. Stir quinoa mixture. Turn off pot. Let quinoa mixture stand. Garnish with parsley.

**NINJA** HEALTHY TIP

Artichokes are a great source of fiber. Stir 1 package (about 9 ounces) frozen artichoke hearts in with the capers in step 3.

 STOVETOP

# FRESH TUNA CASSEROLE

**A fresh and delicious twist on a favorite classic — panko crumbs and fresh tuna make this dish fresh and delicious.**

**PREP:** 5 minutes • **COOK:** 10–15 minutes • **SERVINGS:** 4

## Ingredients

1 10-ounce can cream of mushroom soup

1 bag (10 ounces) frozen vegetable medley

3 cups water

1 12-ounce bag wide egg noodles

1 pound tuna, cubed

salt and pepper to taste

2 tablespoons panko bread crumbs

## Directions

**1.** Set pot to STOVETOP HIGH. Meanwhile, stir together soup, vegetables, and water, then add to pot.

**2.** Stir in egg noodles.

**3.** Place cubed tuna on rack, place rack in pot, cover, and cook 6–10 minutes.

**4.** Remove rack, gently stir cooked tuna into noodle mixture, and season with salt and pepper. Split between four dishes and garnish with bread crumbs.

**NINJA** HEALTHY TIP

Go old school and use canned tuna — just select a high-quality version packed in water and drain well.

STOVETOP/STEAM OVEN

# TACO-INSPIRED BAKED ZITI

Look in the international section of your local supermarket to find the sofrito sauce and the Ro-Tel tomatoes and chilies.

**PREP:** 10 minutes • **COOK:** 16–18 minutes • **SERVINGS:** 4–6

## Ingredients

**1 tablespoon canola oil**

**1 pound ground beef**

**1 packet taco seasoning**

**2 cups water**

**2 cups sofrito sauce**

**2 cans (10 ounces each) Ro-Tel zesty diced tomatoes and green chilies**

**2 tablespoons lime juice**

**8 ounces ziti**

**salt and pepper to taste**

**2 cups low-fat Mexican cheese mix, shredded**

**¼ cup fresh cilantro, chopped for garnish**

## Directions

**1.** Set pot to STOVETOP HIGH and heat canola oil. Add ground beef and taco seasoning, then sauté 4 minutes or until browned.

**2.** Set OVEN to 350°F. Add water, sofrito sauce, tomatoes, lime juice, and ziti. Blend well and cover. Cook 6 minutes.

**3.** Stir once, cover, and cook 6 more minutes.

**4.** Turn off pot. Sprinkle cheese on top, cover, and wait until the cheese has melted. Serve immediately, garnished with cilantro.

**NINJA** SERVING TIP

Serve with a salad of chopped romaine, tomato, black beans, corn, and crushed tortilla chips.

 STOVETOP

# LINGUINE WITH SEAFOOD SAUCE

Fire-roasted tomatoes add just that little extra something to any sauce and works beautifully with the smoked paprika in this recipe.

**PREP:** 5 minutes • **COOK:** 25 minutes • **SERVINGS:** 4

## Ingredients

**5 cups water or seafood stock**

**1 tablespoon minced garlic**

**⅛ teaspoon smoked paprika**

**½ small onion, diced**

**1 can (14.5 ounces) fire-roasted tomatoes**

**1 pound linguine**

**1 pound assorted seafood (clams, calamari, mussels, and shrimp with shells off)**

**salt and pepper to taste**

**¼ cup chopped parsley**

## Directions

**1.** Set pot to STOVETOP HIGH. Add water, garlic, paprika, onion, and tomatoes, then stir and add linguine. Cover and cook 20 minutes. Drain pot.

**2.** Stir, then add seafood medley, stir gently, cover, and cook 5 more minutes.

**3.** Season to taste with salt and pepper.

**4.** Divide among four bowls, and garnish with parsley.

**NINJA** SERVING TIP

Add 2 to 4 ounces of dry white wine for an elegant effervescence

 STOVETOP

# TORTELLINI WITH SAUSAGE ALFREDO

Buying the pre grated cheeses saves time, but if you have a good grater, do your own — you will notice the difference.

**PREP:** 15 minutes • **COOK:** 16–18 minutes • **SERVINGS:** 4-6

## Ingredients

**1 tablespoon olive oil**

**2 cloves garlic, minced**

**1 small onion, chopped**

**4 ounces favorite sausage, crumbled**

**1 jar (15 ounces) Alfredo sauce**

**1 cup water**

**2 pounds frozen cheese tortellini**

**1 7-ounce bag baby spinach**

**½ cup grated Parmesan cheese (optional)**

## Directions

**1.** Set pot to STOVETOP HIGH and heat olive oil. Add garlic, onion, and sausage. Sauté 4 minutes until sausage is brown, stirring occasionally.

**2.** Add Alfredo sauce, water, and tortellini. Stir well and cook, covered, until tortellini is al dente, 10–12 minutes.

**3.** Turn off pot. Add spinach, stir, and cook, covered for 2 minutes.

**4.** Divide among dishes, sprinkle with Parmesan cheese, and serve immediately.

**NINJA** SERVING TIP

Turn this into chicken Alfredo by switching out the sausage with rotisserie chicken meat, and the water with chicken stock.

 **STOVETOP/STEAM OVEN**

# HERB-ROASTED PORK TENDERLOINS & POTATOES

**Cook a delicious complete meal, all in one pot! Since you'll want to make this often, you can vary the flavor by substituting your favorite seasonings for the lemon pepper.**

**PREP:** 5 minutes • **COOK:** 25 minutes • **SERVINGS:** 6

## Ingredients

**1 pound red potatoes, cut in quarters**

**1 large onion, cut into wedges**

**1 pound baby carrots**

**2 tablespoons olive oil**

**1 tablespoon lemon pepper seasoning**

**2 pork tenderloins (about 2½ pounds)**

**1 cup chicken broth**

**2 tablespoons chopped fresh parsley**

## Directions

**1.** Place potatoes, onion, and carrots in bowl. Add 1 tablespoon oil and 1 teaspoon lemon pepper seasoning and toss to coat.

**2.** Rub pork with remaining oil and season with remaining lemon pepper seasoning. Place pork into pot. Set to STOVETOP HIGH. Cook uncovered 10 minutes or until pork is browned on all sides. Remove pork from pot.

**3.** Pour broth into pot. Add potato mixture. Place rack into pot and place pork on rack. Set OVEN to 375°F for 20 minutes, checking after 15 minutes. Cover and cook until pork is cooked through. Remove pork from pot. Let meat rest before slicing.

**4.** Serve pork with potato mixture. Sprinkle with parsley.

**NINJA** TIME-SAVER TIP

Look for baby or small red potatoes and avoid the step of cutting them into quarters.

 STOVETOP

# RAVIOLI WITH MUSHROOM SAUCE

Ravioli is Italy's version of a dumpling, traditionally cut and filled by hand. They are excellent frozen, and fresh varieties can be found in most grocery stores in America.

**PREP:** 10 minutes • **COOK:** 17–19 minutes • **SERVINGS:** 4–6

## Ingredients

**2 tablespoons olive oil**

**½ cup diced onions**

**2 cloves garlic, crushed**

**3 cups vegetable stock**

**1 can (10 ounces) cream of mushroom soup**

**8 ounces mushrooms, sliced**

**2 pounds frozen meat ravioli**

## Directions

**1.** Set pot to STOVETOP HIGH and heat olive oil. Add onion and garlic, and sauté 2 minutes.

**2.** Add stock, soup, and mushrooms, and stir well.

**3.** Slowly add ravioli, then stir gently to coat.

**4.** Cover and cook 15–17 minutes, then serve immediately.

## NINJA SERVING TIP

Garnish with ¼ cup Romano cheese and 1 tablespoon fresh chopped parsley for a tasty topper and a pretty finished dish.

 STOVETOP

# SHRIMP PAD THAI

Pad Thai is an easy and delicious twist for a quick weekday meal. Rice noodles are found in the Asian section of your supermarket.

**PREP:** 20 minutes • **COOK:** 14–16 minutes • **SERVINGS:** 4

## Ingredients

**4 cups water**

**7 ounces dried wide rice noodles**

**¼ cup agave**

**4 tablespoons soy sauce**

**2 tablespoons lime juice**

**4 tablespoons apple cider vinegar**

**3 tablespoons ketchup**

**2 tablespoons sesame oil**

**2 tablespoons olive oil**

**1 pound large shrimp (16–20 count, peeled and deveined)**

**½ cup onion, thinly sliced**

**½ cup celery, thinly sliced**

**1 cup cabbage, sliced into 1-inch strips**

**½ cup chopped peanuts**

**1 lime, cut into 8 wedges**

**4 teaspoons freshly chopped cilantro**

## Directions

**1.** Set pot to STOVETOP HIGH. Add water and bring to a boil. Add noodles and cook 8 minutes. Drain pot.

**2.** Meanwhile, whisk together agave, soy sauce, lime juice, vinegar, ketchup, sesame oil, and olive oil.

**3.** Add agave mixture, shrimp, onion, celery, and cabbage to noodles. Stir to incorporate and cook 6–8 minutes.

**4.** Split among four bowls and garnish with peanuts, lime wedge, and cilantro.

**NINJA** SERVING TIP

Add ½ teaspoon crushed red pepper flakes and 2 tablespoons fish sauce for added heat and a more authentic Thai flavor.

 OVEN

# COD WITH TOMATO CAPER SAUCE & SUGAR SNAP PEAS

The delicate flavor of cod pairs perfectly with the more assertive flavors of capers, garlic, and basil in the sauce. This flavorful liquid keeps the cod moist and helps cook the sugar snap peas to the perfect tender-crisp texture.

**PREP:** 5 minutes • **COOK:** 20 minutes • **SERVINGS:** 4

## Ingredients

**2 medium tomatoes, chopped**

**½ cup white wine**

**2 tablespoons drained capers**

**2 cloves garlic, minced**

**1 tablespoon chopped fresh basil leaves**

**½ teaspoon salt**

**4 cod fillets (about 1 pound)**

**¾ pound sugar snap peas**

## Directions

**1.** Stir tomatoes, wine, capers, garlic, basil, and salt in pot. Add fish to pot. Set OVEN to 375°F for 10 minutes; cover.

**2.** Place snap peas on fish. Cover and cook until fish flakes easily when tested with a fork and snap peas are tender-crisp, about 10 more minutes.

**NINJA** TIME-SAVER TIP

Substitute 1 can (14.5 ounces) diced tomatoes in juice for chopped tomatoes.

 STOVETOP

# CHEDDAR-STUFFED BURGERS WITH BARBECUE DIJON ONIONS

**Simple and inexpensive ingredients combine to create bistro-worthy burgers in 30 minutes. Your family and friends will vote this recipe as one of their favorites.**

**PREP:** 15 minutes  •  **COOK:** 15 minutes  •  **SERVINGS:** 4

## Ingredients

**1 pound lean ground beef**

**4 cubes (1-inch) low-fat Cheddar cheese**

**Salt and ground black pepper**

**2 teaspoons canola oil**

**2 medium onions, chopped**

**¼ cup barbecue sauce**

**1 tablespoon Dijon mustard**

**4 potato sandwich rolls**

## Directions

**1.** Shape beef into 4 burgers. Make an indentation in center of each burger and place 1 piece of cheese in each. Press beef to enclose cheese. Season burgers with salt and black pepper.

**2.** Pour 1 teaspoon oil into pot. Set to STOVETOP HIGH and heat oil. Stir in onions. Cook uncovered 5 minutes or until onions are tender, stirring occasionally. Stir in barbecue sauce and mustard. Cook uncovered 1 minute or until hot. Move onion mixture to one side of pot.

**3.** Add remaining oil and burgers to pot. Cook uncovered 9 minutes or until burgers are cooked through, turning over once halfway through cooking time. Serve burgers and onion mixture on rolls.

**NINJA** TIME-SAVER TIP

Look in your grocer's freezer case for frozen onions already chopped or in the produce section or salad bar.

 STOVETOP/OVEN

# CAVATELLI & BROCCOLI ALFREDO

**This classic Italian dish is made with cavatelli right from the freezer. There's no need to thaw or cook separately — it all cooks right in one pot.**

**PREP:** 5 minutes • **COOK:** 25 minutes • **SERVINGS:** 4

## Ingredients

**1 tablespoon olive oil**

**1 small onion, chopped**

**2 cloves garlic, minced**

**1 package (about 14 ounces) frozen cavatelli**

**4 cups broccoli florets**

**1 jar (15 ounces) light Alfredo sauce**

**2 cups water**

**¼ cup shredded Parmesan cheese**

## Directions

**1.** Pour oil into pot. Set to STOVETOP HIGH and heat oil. Stir in onion and garlic. Cook uncovered 5 minutes or until onion is tender, stirring occasionally.

**2.** Stir in cavatelli, broccoli, sauce, and water. Set to OVEN to 350°F. Cover and cook 20 minutes or until cavatelli and broccoli are tender. Stir in cheese just before serving.

**NINJA** SERVING TIP

Frozen tortellini can replace cavatelli, and asparagus and roasted red peppers can replace broccoli for an alternative dish. Adding ¼ cup diced prosciutto also makes a tasty variation.

 STOVETOP

# HONEY-MUSTARD CHICKEN

If you enjoy the fast-food chicken tenders with honey-mustard dipping sauce, this is the healthier chicken weekday option for you and your family.

**PREP:** 5 minutes • **COOK:** 18 minutes • **SERVINGS:** 4

## Ingredients

**¼ cup canola oil**

**½ cup honey**

**¼ cup Dijon mustard**

**4 4-ounce chicken breasts**

**salt and pepper to taste**

**1 cup panko bread crumbs**

## Directions

**1.** Set pot to STOVETOP HIGH and add canola oil. Meanwhile, whisk together honey and mustard.

**2.** Season chicken breasts with salt and pepper. Coat chicken in mustard mixture and then in bread crumbs.

**3.** Add chicken breasts, set pot to STOVETOP LOW, cook 9 minutes, flip chicken, and cook 9 more minutes.

**4.** Remove chicken and serve immediately.

**NINJA** HEALTHY TIP

Slice and serve over Caesar salad — no need for croutons with this crispy chicken.

 STEAM OVEN

# SALMON WITH CREAMY ORZO PESTO

While orzo looks like rice, it is actually pasta cut to look like rice; in English it translates to barley.

**PREP:** 12 minutes • **COOK:** 12–14 minutes • **SERVINGS:** 4

## Ingredients

**4 4-ounce salmon fillets**

**½ teaspoon salt**

**¼ teaspoon pepper**

**4 cups chicken stock**

**½ cup orzo**

**½ cup peas, frozen**

**2 tablespoons pesto, plus 4 teaspoons pesto**

**¼ cup Parmesan cheese**

**¼ cup plain Greek yogurt**

**fresh basil**

## Directions

1. Season salmon with salt and pepper and place on rack.

2. Set pot to STOVETOP HIGH. Add chicken stock, stir in orzo and peas. Place rack with salmon on top of orzo. Cover and cook 12–14 minutes.

3. Remove rack. Stir 2 tablespoons pesto, Parmesan cheese, and yogurt into orzo.

4. Split orzo among four dishes and top with salmon. Top each portion with 1 teaspoon pesto and garnish with fresh basil.

**NINJA** SERVING TIP

Use your favorite pesto recipe for the freshest flavor in this dish.

STOVETOP/OVEN

# CHICKEN POT PIE

This inverted chicken pot pie surprises with a crisp crust on the bottom that becomes the top when scooped out.

**PREP:** 5 minutes • **COOK:** 20–25 minutes • **SERVINGS:** 4

## Ingredients

**1 refrigerated pie crust**

**1 12-ounce bag frozen vegetables**

**1 pound cooked chicken, diced**

**1 can (10.75 ounces) can condensed cream of chicken soup**

**4 ounces water**

**1 cup chopped celery**

## Directions

**1.** Unroll one crust and press in bottom and up the sides of pot.

**2.** Set pot to STOVETOP HIGH. Meanwhile, stir together remaining ingredients.

**3.** Pour vegetable mixture on top of pie crust. Set pot to OVEN 350°F. Cover and cook 20–25 minutes.

**4.** Crust should be a beautiful golden brown. Scoop and serve immediately.

**NINJA** SERVING TIP

In place of cream of chicken soup, use cream of celery soup for an extra layer of flavor.

 STOVETOP

# PARSNIP, LEEK, & FONTINA ALFREDO

**A savory and easy holiday side dish or easy light vegetarian dinner casserole.**

**PREP:** 5 minutes • **COOK:** 25 minutes • **SERVINGS:** 4–6

## Ingredients

**2 tablespoons olive oil**

**2 pounds parsnips, cut into ½-inch pieces**

**3 leeks, thinly sliced**

**1 cup bread crumbs**

**4 ounces fontina cheese, grated**

**3 tablespoons coarsely chopped flat-leaf parsley**

**kosher salt and pepper to taste**

## Directions

**1.** Set pot to STOVETOP HIGH and heat oil. Add parsnips and leeks to pot, stirring occasionally. Cook approximately 20 minutes or until just tender.

**2.** Stir in bread crumbs, cheese, and parsley. Cook 5 minutes, stirring occasionally.

**3.** Season with salt and pepper, taste, and adjust seasonings.

 SERVING TIP

Serve with a side salad for a complete meal.

**SEA BASS Á LA NAGE WITH STEAMED ROMAINE**

# CHAPTER 2:
# Lite Fare

# APRICOT & COUNTRY MUSTARD SALMON

The liquid in the bottom of the pot keeps the salmon moist and flavorful. This dish has amazing flavor, and it's surprisingly easy to make — with ingredients right from your pantry.

**PREP:** 5 minutes • **COOK:** 10 minutes • **SERVINGS:** 4

## Ingredients

2 cups water

¼ cup apricot preserves

2 tablespoons country Dijon-style mustard

1½ pounds salmon fillets

salt and ground black pepper

## Directions

**1.** Pour water into pot and set dial to to STEAMER. Set timer to 20 minutes and wait for the beep.

**2.** Meanwhile stir preserves and mustard in bowl.

**3.** Season fish with salt and pepper. Place fish on rack. Spread preserve mixture on fish.

**4.** When beep sounds, use oven mitts to carefully place rack into pot and cover, checking after 10–15 minutes for desired doneness.

**5.** With oven mitts, carefully remove rack from pot.

 SERVING TIP

Sprinkle the fish with sliced green onion and serve with baked potatoes and a green salad.

# HOT & SOUR SHRIMP SAUTÉ

Forget take-out — this restaurant-worthy recipe is ready in 25 minutes! When buying fresh ginger, use a 1-inch peeled piece to make the minced tablespoon needed here. Wrap what's left and store it in the freezer for several months.

**PREP:** 15 minutes  •  **COOK:** 10 minutes  •  **SERVINGS:** 4

## Ingredients

1 tablespoon packed brown sugar

1 tablespoon cornstarch

¾ cup water or vegetable broth

3 tablespoons rice wine vinegar

2 tablespoons soy sauce

1 tablespoon vegetable oil

¾ pound uncooked medium shrimp, peeled and deveined

1 tablespoon minced fresh ginger

2 cloves garlic, minced

¼ teaspoon crushed red pepper

1 package (about 3.5 ounces) sliced shiitake mushrooms

1 large red bell pepper, cut into thin strips

3 green onions, finely chopped

## Directions

1. Stir brown sugar and cornstarch in bowl. Add water, vinegar, and soy sauce and stir until smooth.

2. Pour oil into pot. Set to STOVETOP HIGH and heat oil. Add shrimp, ginger, garlic, and crushed red pepper. Cook uncovered 2 minutes. Add mushrooms and bell pepper. Cook 2 minutes, stirring occasionally.

3. Stir in vinegar mixture. Cover and cook 2 minutes or until shrimp are cooked through, stirring occasionally. Stir in green onions. Serve shrimp mixture over rice.

**NINJA** SERVING TIP

Serve the shrimp mixture over hot cooked white rice or rice noodles.

 STEAMER

# HALIBUT WITH SWISS CHARD

Talk about healthy! Fresh fish is good for the brain, while Swiss chard contains healthy doses of magnesium, vitamin A, and vitamin C.

**PREP:** 20 minutes • **COOK:** 10–12 minutes • **SERVINGS:** 4

## Ingredients

1 tablespoon lemon juice

1 cup white wine

1 cup water

1 tablespoon butter

4 4-ounce halibut fillets

salt and pepper to taste

4 large leaves Swiss chard, stems chopped and reserved

2 teaspoons lemon zest

4 teaspoons finely chopped shallots

1 clove garlic, minced

## Directions

1. Add lemon juice, wine, water, and butter to pot.

2. Set dial to STEAMER. Set timer to 12 minutes and wait for beep.

3. Meanwhile, season halibut with salt and pepper. Lay out one large leaf of Swiss chard, greenest side down, and put one halibut in center of leaf. Top with ½ teaspoon lemon zest, 1 teaspoon shallot, a pinch of minced garlic, and ¼ of the chopped Swiss chard stems.

4. Gently fold the leaf of Swiss chard over and around halibut to create a "package." Repeat steps 3 and 4 for remaining halibut fillets. Arrange all fillets on steamer rack.

5. When beep sounds, use oven mitts to carefully place rack into the pot and cover, checking after 10 minutes for desired doneness.

6. With oven mitts carefully remove rack from pot. Transfer packages to plates, and top with wine-butter sauce.

**NINJA** SERVING TIP

Add 1 teaspoon of orange marmalade to the center of each package in step 3 to create a sweet-layered citrus finish.

 **STOVETOP**

# MOROCCAN SALMON

You will like this easy dish so much, you will keep plenty of this spice mix on hand so you are ready to go.

**PREP:** 5 minutes • **COOK:** 8–12 minutes • **SERVINGS:** 4

## Ingredients

**Spice Mix:**

> 1 teaspoon cinnamon
>
> 1 teaspoon ginger
>
> 1 teaspoon mustard
>
> 1 teaspoon cumin
>
> ½ teaspoon salt
>
> ¼ teaspoon black pepper

4 6-ounce salmon fillets

## Directions

1. Set pot to STOVETOP HIGH and add canola oil. Meanwhile, mix together spice mix ingredients and coat salmon fillets with it.

2. Add salmon. Sear on one side 4–6 minutes, flip salmon, sear 4–6 minutes more, and serve immediately.

**NINJA** SERVING TIP

Top each salmon fillet with 1 tablespoon of harissa sauce and really impress your friends who like it spicy.

STOVETOP

# PORK CHOPS WITH PEAR CHUTNEY

Pears are one of those fruits that are picked unripe; they are then stored and allowed to ripen off the tree. If your pear is rock hard, it is not ripe. It is best to store it in a cool, dark space until the skin changes color.

**PREP:** 12 minutes • **COOK:** 22–31 minutes • **SERVINGS:** 4

## Ingredients

1 tablespoon olive oil

1 tablespoon cardamom

1 tablespoon coriander

1 tablespoon cinnamon

salt and pepper

4 3-ounce pork chops

1 cup baby carrots

¼ cup champagne vinegar

4 tablespoons brown sugar

½ cup water

1 pear, cored, diced ½ inch

## Directions

1. Set pot to STOVETOP HIGH and add olive oil. Meanwhile, season pork chops with cardamom, coriander, cinnamon, salt, and pepper.

2. Add pork chops, sear 2–3 minutes to brown, flip, and sear 2–3 minutes more.

3. Add carrots and sauté 3–5 minutes, stirring occasionally.

4. Whisk together vinegar and brown sugar to dissolve the brown sugar a bit, then whisk in water.

5. Add liquid and pears, and cook 15–20 minutes, stirring occasionally. Chutney will thicken. Serve immediately.

**NINJA** SERVING TIP

Invest in your pantry. Get the best-quality dried spices and vinegars you can afford by going to a specialty store.

STOVETOP

# TURKEY BURGERS

Baby portabellas add a beeflike texture and taste to these awesome turkey burgers.

**PREP:** 15 minutes • **COOK:** 11- 15 minutes • **SERVINGS:** 8

## Ingredients

2 tablespoons olive oil

½ cup minced onion

1 cup chopped baby portabella mushrooms

1 clove garlic, minced

2 pounds ground turkey

1 teaspoon ground mustard

salt and pepper to taste

1 large egg

⅓ cup panko bread crumbs

¼ head iceberg lettuce, shredded

8 tomato slices

8 hamburger buns

## Directions

1. Set pot to STOVETOP HIGH and add 1 tablespoon olive oil. Add onion, mushrooms, and garlic. Sauté 3 minutes, then remove to a large bowl.

2. Mix vegetable mixture with ground turkey, mustard, salt, pepper, egg, and bread crumbs. Form eight ½-inch burgers.

3. Add remaining olive oil. Add four burgers and sear, then cover and cook 4–6 minutes. Flip, sear, cover, and cook 4–6 minutes more.

4. Remove burgers and keep warm. Repeat step 3 for the remaining four burgers.

5. Serve burgers on buns with tomato and lettuce.

**NINJA** SERVING TIP

Add 2 teaspoons fresh sage to your burger mix in step 2, than slather your bun with cranberry chutney for an instant Thanksgiving throwback.

**Lite Fare**

# COD WITH SAUCE VIERGE

Sauce vierge is of French origin, a lovely sauce for light-flavored fish; it is like a chunky, tangy warm vinaigrette.

**PREP:** 12 minutes • **COOK:** 15–20 minutes • **SERVINGS:** 4

## Ingredients

¼ cup olive oil

½ cup chopped onions

1 cup diced plum tomatoes

1 teaspoon coriander

1 tablespoon balsamic vinegar

4 5-ounce cod fillets

salt and pepper to taste

1 tablespoon chopped basil

¼ cup chopped cilantro

## Directions

1. Set pot to STOVETOP HIGH and add olive oil.

2. Add onions, tomatoes, coriander, and vinegar, then stir to incorporate.

3. Set dial to STEAMER . Set timer to 15 minutes and wait for beep.

4. Meanwhile, season cod with salt and pepper, and place on rack.

5. When beep sounds, use oven mitts to carefully place rack into the pot and cover, checking after 10 minutes for desired doneness.

6. With oven mitts, carefully remove rack from pot. And stir basil and cilantro into sauce.

7. Divide sauce among plates, top with cod, and serve immediately.

**NINJA** SERVING TIP

Serve over angel hair pasta tossed with haricots verts for a fabulous and beautiful meal.

 STOVETOP

# SEARED STRIP STEAK WITH BALSAMIC ONIONS

Ah, dinner for two! Have date night at home with this quick and easy dish, simple but impressively delicious.

**PREP:** 5 minutes • **COOK:** 12–14 minutes • **SERVINGS:** 2

## Ingredients

2 tablespoons olive oil

2 6-ounce strip steaks

salt and pepper to taste

1 medium yellow onion, cut in half, then sliced ¼ inch lengthwise

¼ cup balsamic vinegar

1 teaspoon sugar

## Directions

1. Set pot to STOVETOP HIGH and add olive oil.

2. Season steaks with salt and pepper.

3. Add onion slices, stirring to coat with oil, cover, and cook 3 minutes.

4. Add sugar and stir until dissolved, about 1 minute.

5. Add vinegar and stir to incorporate.

6. Remove onions and keep warm in foil-covered dish.

7. Add steaks and sear 4- 5 minutes. Flip steaks, top with onions, and cook 4–5 minutes. Serve immediately.

**NINJA** SERVING TIP

Serve with the traditional steak house wedge salad: iceberg, crumbled bacon, blue cheese, diced tomato, diced red onion, and blue cheese dressing.

# SEA BASS Á LA NAGE WITH STEAMED ROMAINE

This dish is healthful yet packed with flavor. The fish and romaine are layered in the pot and cook at the same time, while the sauce cooks in the bottom. It's perfect for a summer dinner party.

**PREP:** 15 minutes • **COOK:** 15 minutes • **SERVINGS:** 4

## Ingredients

1 lemon

4 sea bass fillets, skin removed (about 1 pound)

salt and ground black pepper

3 tablespoons butter

1 tablespoon minced shallot

2 garlic cloves, minced

½ cup white wine

½ cup chicken stock

2 hearts of romaine, cut in half lengthwise

2 teaspoons sliced fresh chives

## Directions

1. Grate zest and squeeze juice from lemon. Season fish with salt and ground black pepper.

2. Place butter into pot. Set to STOVETOP HIGH and heat until butter is melted. Add shallot and garlic to pot. Cook uncovered 1 minute. Stir in wine and cook 2 minutes or until slightly reduced. Stir in stock and lemon zest and season with salt and black pepper.

3. Place fish on rack and place rack into pot. Place romaine on top of fish. Season with salt and black pepper. Set OVEN to 425°F for 10 minutes. Cover and cook until fish flakes easily when tested with a fork and romaine is tender-crisp.

4. Remove rack with fish and romaine from pot. Stir lemon juice into pot. Serve romaine topped with fish and drizzled with stock mixture. Sprinkle with chives.

**NINJA** SERVING TIP

Use whichever white wine you prefer in this recipe, and serve the rest with dinner! Chardonnay will lend a more buttery flavor, while Riesling will add a sweeter, more fruity note.

# SPAGHETTI SQUASH WITH TURKEY SAUSAGE

The flesh of cooked spaghetti squash separates into shreds resembling thin spaghetti, making it a great alternative to cooked pasta. Sausage cooks in the pot, then the squash is baked until tender and the "spaghetti" can be scraped out.

**PREP:** 10 minutes • **COOK:** 50 minutes • **SERVINGS:** 6

## Ingredients

1 pound Italian-style turkey sausage, casing removed

2 cups water

1 large spaghetti squash (about 4 pounds), cut in half lengthwise and seeds removed

2 tablespoons grated Parmesan cheese

2 teaspoons no-salt garlic and herb seasoning

1 large tomato, chopped

1 cup packed baby spinach leaves

¼ cup shredded mozzarella cheese

## Directions

1. Set pot to STOVETOP HIGH. Add sausage to pot. Cook uncovered 10 minutes or until browned, stirring often. Remove sausage from pot. Spoon off fat.

2. Pour water into pot. Place rack into pot. Place squash, cut side down, on rack. Set OVEN to 425°F for 25 minutes. Cover and cook until squash is tender. Remove squash and rack from pot and let cool 5 minutes.

3. Using fork, scrape flesh from squash and add to pot. Sprinkle with 1 tablespoon Parmesan cheese and 1 teaspoon garlic and herb seasoning. Top with sausage, tomato, spinach, and remaining Parmesan cheese and seasoning. Set OVEN to 425°F for 15 minutes. Cover and cook until mixture is hot and bubbling. Sprinkle with mozzarella cheese.

**NINJA** SERVING TIP

Delicious topped with fresh ground or cracked black pepper.

 **STOVETOP**

# TEQUILA SCALLOPS WITH CHILI & CILANTRO

Make sure you dry scallops before you start cooking; it is the trick to great searing.

**PREP:** 15 minutes • **COOK:** 10–12 minutes • **SERVINGS:** 4

## Ingredients

1½ pounds sea scallops

2 tablespoons olive oil

salt and pepper

1 jalapeño pepper, seeded, membrane removed, thinly sliced

1 poblano pepper, seeded, membrane removed, thinly sliced

½ cubanelle pepper, seeded, membrane removed, thinly sliced

¼ cup tequila

2 tablespoons chopped cilantro

¼ cup chopped tomato

## Directions

1. Pat scallops between paper towels to dry and season with salt and pepper.

2. Set pot to STOVETOP HIGH and add 1 tablespoon olive oil.

3. Add scallops and sear 3 minutes. Flip and sear 3 more minutes to brown. Remove and keep warm.

4. Add 1 tablespoon olive oil to pot, and heat oil.

5. Add peppers and sauté 2 minutes.

6. Add tequila and stir.

7. Add scallops and cilantro. Cover and cook 2 minutes.

8. Split between four plates and top each serving with 1 tablespoon of chopped tomato.

**NINJA** SERVING TIP

Serve with fresh arugula tossed in olive oil and lemon juice, and finish with shredded Locatelli cheese.

# PISTACHIO-CRUSTED SWORDFISH

Pistachios are a great addition of flavor and protein. Perfect for low-carb diets!

**PREP:** 10 minutes • **COOK:** 6–8 minutes • **SERVINGS:** 4

## Ingredients

4 6-ounce swordfish steaks

2 tablespoons canola oil

2 teaspoons chopped parsley

1 cup chopped pistachios

salt and pepper to taste

4 teaspoons Dijon mustard

## Directions

1. Set pot to STOVETOP HIGH and add oil.

2. Mix parsley, pistachios, salt, and pepper together.

3. Spread 1 teaspoon of mustard on top of each swordfish steak.

4. Sprinkle pistachio mixture on top of mustard, pressing evenly to form a crust.

5. Add fish pistachio side down and sear 3–4 minutes. Flip, then sear 3–4 minutes more until golden brown. Serve immediately.

**NINJA** SERVING TIP

You can also substitute half of the pistachios with panko bread crumbs if you want a less intense pistachio flavor.

 **STOVETOP/STEAMER**

# GNOCCHI WITH BROCCOLI RABE

Comfort food is so convenient when you make it in one pot and have fewer pans to clean up. Use leftovers to create variations on this tasty theme.

**PREP:** 5 minutes • **COOK:** 10–14 minutes • **SERVINGS:** 4

## Ingredients

1 bunch broccoli rabe, trimmed and chopped

5 cups water, divided

16 ounces gnocchi, fresh

1 tablespoon olive oil

1 clove garlic, sliced

½ cup chicken stock

salt and pepper to taste

¼ cup Parmesan cheese, shaved

## Directions

1. Add 1 cup water to pot. Set pot to STEAMER, and set timer for 3 minutes and wait for beep.

2. Meanwhile, place broccoli rabe on the rack. When beep sounds, carefully place rack into the pot with oven mitts and cover.

3. After 3 minutes check for desired doneness. Using oven mitts, carefully remove rack from pot. Remove broccoli rabe warm in foil-covered bowl.

4. Set to STOVETOP HIGH, add 4 cups of water, and bring to a boil. Add gnocchi and cook 4 minutes. Turn off pot and drain.

5. Set pot to STOVETOP HIGH, add olive oil and garlic, and sauté 2-4 minutes, stirring occasionally.

6. Add broccoli rabe, gnocchi, and chicken stock and cook 2-4 minutes, stirring occasionally.

7. Season with salt and pepper, top with shaved cheese, and serve immediately.

**NINJA** SERVING TIP

For another great meal, add 2 cups of cooked shrimp. Simply add in at step 5 after sautéing garlic.

◎ ▦ **STOVETOP/OVEN**

# HERB-INFUSED TURKEY BREAST

A healthier holiday can include serving turkey breast as your entrée. Preparing the breast in an herb- and vegetable-infused broth adds juiciness and delicious flavors to your meal.

**PREP:** 20 minutes • **COOK:** 1 hour • **SERVINGS:** 6–8

## Ingredients

1 5–6 pound turkey breast

3 carrots, peeled and cut into ½-inch disks

1 onion, peeled and chopped

2 ribs celery, cut into ½-inch slices

kosher salt and pepper

4 cups chicken broth

5 sprigs fresh thyme

3 sprigs fresh rosemary

1 lemon, juiced

½ teaspoon chili powder (optional)

## Directions

1. Set to STOVETOP HIGH and heat pot for 5 minutes. Add carrots, onion, and celery and sauté until translucent 2–3 minutes. Season with salt and pepper and brown turkey breast on both sides, stirring vegetables occasionally, about 10 minutes on each side.

2. Add chicken broth, thyme, and rosemary sprigs and squeeze lemon over breast (straining seeds). Sprinkle chili powder over breast (optional).

3. Cover and set OVEN to 375°F for 1 hour or until breast is cooked through.

4. Remove turkey, slice, and serve with vegetables and jus.

**NINJA** SERVING TIP

After removing the thyme and rosemary sprigs from the cooker, set to STOVETOP HIGH. Add 4 cups chicken or turkey broth mixed with 1 tablespoon cornstarch, to make a delicious chicken gravy in just about 5 minutes.

**PULLED PORK & APPLE CIDER SLIDERS**

# CHAPTER 3: Appetizers

 STOVETOP

# WARM & SPICY WHITE BEAN & ARTICHOKE DIP

**This rich, Tuscan-inspired dip is simple to make with ingredients right from your pantry.**

**PREP:** 15 minutes  •  **COOK:** 25 minutes  •  **SERVINGS:** 36

## Ingredients

**2 tablespoons olive oil**

**2 medium onions, diced**

**4 cloves garlic, minced**

**2 packages (8 ounces each) Neufchâtel or light cream cheese, cut up**

**2 cans (9 ounces each) artichoke hearts, drained and coarsely chopped**

**2 cans (about 15 ounces each) cannellini beans, rinsed, drained, and coarsely mashed**

**½ cup milk**

**2 teaspoons cayenne pepper sauce**

**½ cup grated Parmesan cheese**

**salt and ground black pepper**

**1 tablespoon chopped fresh parsley (optional)**

## Directions

**1.** Pour oil into pot. Set to STOVETOP HIGH and heat oil. Add onions to pot. Cook uncovered 5 minutes or until onions are tender, stirring often. Add garlic to pot. Cook 2 minutes, stirring constantly.

**2.** Stir cream cheese, artichokes, beans, milk, and pepper sauce into pot. Set to STOVETOP LOW. Cover and cook 10 minutes or until cream cheese is melted, stirring occasionally. Stir in Parmesan cheese. Season with salt and black pepper. Sprinkle with parsley, if desired.

**NINJA** SERVING TIP

Serve warm with assorted fresh vegetables and/or crackers.

 SLOW COOK

# PULLED PORK & APPLE CIDER SLIDERS

Slow cooking guarantees tender pork. Braised with cider and spicy mustard, these pulled pork sliders make indulgent little sandwiches that are perfect served with baked sweet potato fries.

**PREP:** 10 minutes • **COOK:** 5 hours • **SERVINGS:** 6

## Ingredients

1 boneless pork shoulder roast (3 to 4 pounds)

salt and ground black pepper

2 teaspoons paprika

¼ cup spicy brown mustard

¼ cup packed brown sugar

3 cloves garlic, minced

1 cup apple cider or apple juice

1 package (15 ounces) slider or mini sandwich buns (12 mini buns)

## Directions

**1.** Season pork with salt, black pepper, and paprika. Stir mustard, brown sugar, garlic, and cider in pot. Add pork and turn to coat. Set to SLOW COOK HIGH for 5–6 hours. Cover and cook until pork is fork-tender.

**2.** Transfer pork into large bowl. Using two forks, shred pork. Spread additional mustard on buns, if desired. Divide pork mixture among buns.

**NINJA** TIME-SAVER TIP

Keep this meal quick and simple and serve with sweet potato fries from the freezer section and sliced fresh cucumber with ranch dressing for dipping.

 STOVETOP

# MUSSELS WITH CHORIZO

Chorizo can be sweet or spicy. Pick the type you like, but use either cured or smoked so it is already cooked.

**PREP:** 10 minutes • **COOK:** 10 minutes • **SERVINGS:** 4

## Ingredients

1 pound mussels, cleaned and debearded

½ medium onion, sliced

½ pound chorizo sausage, sliced on bias

1 garlic clove, sliced

1 cup white wine

2 cups water

½ stick butter, cubed

salt and pepper to taste

2 tablespoons chopped cilantro

## Directions

1. Set pot to STOVETOP HIGH and add all the ingredients, except cilantro. Stir and cook 10 minutes.

2. Turn off pot. Use a ladle to dish out so you get all the sauce and sprinkle with cilantro.

**NINJA** SERVING TIP

Have a little more time? Sauté the onions in the butter to caramelize them before adding the other ingredients; you will find it's time well spent.

 **STOVETOP**

# HOT BUFFALO CHICKEN DIP

**Buffalo chicken wings are a favorite with everyone, but they are a mess to eat. Stay clean with this recipe; no Wet-Nap needed.**

**PREP:** 15 minutes • **COOK:** 28 minutes • **SERVINGS:** 6–8

## Ingredients

**1 teaspoon canola oil**

**1 package (8 ounces) cream cheese, softened**

**4 ounces blue cheese, crumbled**

**½ cup blue cheese dressing**

**1 cup sofrito sauce**

**1 teaspoon smoked paprika**

**1 chicken breast, 6 to 8 ounces, cubed into ¼-inch pieces**

## Directions

**1.** Set pot to STOVETOP HIGH and add oil.

**2.** Mix together the cream cheese, blue cheese, blue cheese dressing, sofrito sauce, and paprika and set aside.

**3.** Add chicken and sauté 8 minutes. Cover and stir occasionally.

**4.** Remove chicken and stir into cheese mixture.

**5.** Pour mixture into the roasting pan, place pan in pot, set on STOVETOP LOW, and cook 20 minutes.

**NINJA** SERVING TIP

Serve with veggies or your favorite crackers. Try adding some chopped celery and carrot to the mixture in step 2.

 STOVETOP

# CRAB IMPERIAL WITH ARTICHOKE CROSTINI

Traditionally, Crab Imperial is baked and served in a scallop shell, but you cannot eat that, so try serving it on a crostini instead.

**PREP:** 10 minutes • **COOK:** 40–45 minutes • **SERVINGS:** 40

## Ingredients

**24 ounces cream cheese, softened**

**½ cup sour cream**

**2 tablespoons lemon juice**

**3 tablespoons Worcestershire sauce**

**2 tablespoons Old Bay seasoning**

**1 jar (14 ounces) artichokes, quartered, drained**

**1 pound lump crab**

**40 crostini**

## Directions

**1.** Set pot to STOVETOP LOW.

**2.** Mix together all ingredients except crabmeat.

**3.** Gently fold in crabmeat and put in pot.

**4.** Cook 40–45 minutes.

**5.** Turn off pot. Spoon mixture onto crostini and serve immediately.

**NINJA** HEALTHY TIP

For a lower-fat option, try using fat-free sour cream and fat-free cream cheese.

**Appetizers**

# BROCCOLI CHEESE DIP

This is no ordinary broccoli dip! Sautéed onion provides a savory base, then broccoli, cheese, and seasonings slow cook until the mixture is hot and the flavors are blended. A bit of sun-dried tomato pesto adds the perfect tasty twist.

**PREP:** 10 minutes • **COOK:** 2 hours, 10 minutes • **SERVINGS:** 6

## Ingredients

**1 tablespoon olive oil**

**1 medium onion, chopped**

**4 cups chopped fresh broccoli**

**1 can (10.75 ounces) condensed broccoli cheese soup**

**½ cup milk**

**1 tablespoon Worcestershire sauce**

**1 tablespoon sun-dried tomato pesto sauce**

**1 cup shredded Cheddar cheese**

**ground black pepper**

## Directions

**1.** Pour oil into pot. Set to STOVETOP HIGH and heat oil. Add onion to pot. Cook uncovered 5 minutes or until onion is tender-crisp, stirring occasionally. Add broccoli to pot. Cook 5 minutes, stirring occasionally.

**2.** Stir soup, milk, Worcestershire, pesto sauce, cheese, and black pepper into pot. Set to SLOW COOK LOW for 2 hours. Cover and cook until broccoli is tender and cheese is melted.

**NINJA** HEALTHY TIP

Substitute reduced-fat broccoli cheese soup and 2% milk Cheddar cheese for the versions in the recipe.

 **STOVETOP**

# SPICED NUTS

Mixed nuts are glazed with a spicy brown sugar coating and sprinkled with fresh orange zest. The pot's nonstick surface makes cleanup fuss-free.

**PREP:** 2 minutes • **COOK:** 5 minutes • **SERVINGS:** 10

## Ingredients

**1 orange**

**1 can (10 ounces) mixed nuts**

**2 tablespoons canola oil**

**2 tablespoons packed light brown sugar**

**½ teaspoon cayenne pepper**

**¼ teaspoon ground cumin**

**1 teaspoon cinnamon**

**1 tablespoon water**

## Directions

**1.** Grate zest from orange and place in a small bowl. Line a rimmed baking sheet with parchment paper.

**2.** Place nuts, oil, brown sugar, cayenne, cumin, cinnamon, and water into pot and set to STOVETOP HIGH. Cook uncovered 5 minutes or until sugar is melted and the sugar mixture coats the nuts, stirring constantly.

**3.** Spread nut mixture on baking sheet. Sprinkle with orange zest. Let stand 10 minutes or until sugar mixture is hardened.

**NINJA** SERVING TIP

Serve as a casual bite while watching the game or as an upscale snack for a cocktail party.

**Appetizers**

# CHICKEN SATAY

In only 25 minutes you will have seasoned chicken skewers ready for dipping into a beautiful creamy sauce cooked at the same time!

**PREP:** 10 minutes • **COOK:** 15 minutes • **SERVINGS:** 8

## Ingredients

**16 wooden skewers**

**cooking spray**

**1 pound boneless, skinless chicken tenderloins, cut in half lengthwise**

**¼ teaspoon cayenne pepper**

**½ teaspoon ground ginger**

**Salt and ground black pepper**

**2 tablespoons canola oil**

**2 cloves garlic, minced**

**1 can (14 ounces) coconut milk**

**3 tablespoons creamy peanut butter**

**1½ tablespoons reduced-sodium soy sauce**

**3 tablespoons packed light brown sugar**

**fresh cilantro leaves**

## Directions

**1.** Spray skewers with cooking spray. Thread chicken onto skewers. Season with cayenne pepper, ginger, salt, and black pepper.

**2.** Add oil and garlic to pot. Set to STOVETOP HIGH. Cook uncovered 1 minute or until garlic is tender, stirring often. Stir coconut milk, peanut butter, soy sauce, and brown sugar into pot. Season with salt and black pepper.

**3.** Place skewers on rack. Place rack into pot. Set OVEN to 325°F for 10 minutes, checking after 5 minutes. Cover and cook until chicken is cooked through. Remove skewers from pot, cover, and keep warm.

**4.** Cook coconut milk mixture uncovered 5 minutes or until thickened, stirring often. Serve skewers with sauce for dipping. Sprinkle with cilantro.

**NINJA** HEALTHY TIP

Substitute reduced-fat broccoli cheese soup, skim milk, and 2% milk Cheddar cheese for a lighter version.

 STOVETOP

# WILD MUSHROOM CROSTINI

Sautéing in the pot enhances the earthy flavor of the mushrooms, which are finished with Marsala wine and basil. Serve on crusty bread slices with a sprinkle of Parmesan cheese.

**PREP:** 10 minutes • **COOK:** 15 minutes • **SERVINGS:** 8

## Ingredients

**2 tablespoons butter**

**10 ounces assorted fresh wild mushrooms, sliced (cremini, shiitake, oyster, white)**

**2 shallots, minced**

**1 clove garlic, minced**

**½ teaspoon sea salt**

**⅛ teaspoon freshly ground black pepper**

**2 tablespoons Marsala wine**

**2 tablespoons finely chopped fresh basil leaves plus 16 small whole fresh basil leaves**

**16 slices (½-inch-thick) French or Italian bread**

**2 tablespoons finely shredded Parmesan cheese**

## Directions

**1.** Place butter into pot. Set to STOVETOP HIGH and heat until butter is melted. Add mushrooms and shallots. Cook uncovered 10 minutes or until mushrooms are lightly browned, stirring occasionally. Add garlic, salt, and black pepper. Cook 1 minute. Stir in wine. Cook 2 minutes or until wine is absorbed, stirring constantly. Stir in chopped basil.

**2.** Spoon about 1 tablespoon mushroom mixture onto each bread slice. Sprinkle with cheese and top each with 1 whole basil leaf.

### NINJA TIME-SAVER TIP

Mushroom mixture can be made a day ahead and refrigerated. Simply reheat in pot on STOVETOP LOW, stirring occasionally, until hot.

 STOVETOP

# PRETZEL-COATED CHICKEN TENDERS

This twist on chicken fingers features a crunchy pretzel coating and a decadent cheesy sauce for dipping. The chicken cooks up crisp on the outside and juicy on the inside, and you make the sauce in the pot, too! Only one pot to clean!

**PREP:** 10 minutes • **COOK:** 15 minutes • **SERVINGS:** 8

## Ingredients

**1 egg**

**2 cups butter-flavored pretzels, finely crushed**

**1 pound boneless chicken breast tenderloins**

**2 tablespoons vegetable oil**

**¾ cup beer or chicken broth**

**8 ounces low-fat Cheddar cheese, cut up**

**1 teaspoon Worcestershire sauce**

**1 teaspoon spicy brown mustard**

## Directions

1. Beat egg in shallow dish. Pour pretzel crumbs onto plate. Dip chicken into egg. Coat chicken with pretzel crumbs.

2. Pour oil into pot. Set to STOVETOP HIGH and heat oil. Add chicken to pot. Cook uncovered 10 minutes or until chicken is browned on both sides and cooked through. Remove chicken from pot, lightly cover, and keep warm.

3. Pour beer into pot and heat to a boil. Add cheese, Worcestershire sauce, and mustard. Cook uncovered until cheese is melted and mixture is smooth, stirring often. Serve sauce with chicken.

## NINJA SERVING TIP

Try cutting the chicken into bite-sized pieces before coating and cooking, then serve on a platter with wooden picks.

STOVETOP/SLOW COOK

# TAILGATE THAI WINGS

Sweet chili sauce is a great Thai condiment that packs in flavor. Look for it in the international aisle at your local grocery store.

**PREP:** 5 minutes • **COOK:** 3 hours, 5 minutes • **SERVINGS:** 4

## Ingredients

**2 pounds chicken wings, tips removed**

**1½ cups prepared sweet chili sauce divided (available in the Asian aisle in most grocery stores)**

**3 scallions, thinly sliced**

## Directions

**1.** Marinate wings for 2 hours to overnight in refrigerator in ¾ cup sweet chili sauce.

**2.** Set pot to STOVETOP HIGH. Put chicken into pot and discard marinade. Cook uncovered 7 minutes on each side or until chicken is browned on both sides.

**3.** Pour remaining sweet chili sauce over chicken and toss to coat. Set to SLOW COOK LOW for 2½–3 hours. Cover and cook until chicken is tender and cooked through.

**4.** To serve, garnish with scallions.

**NINJA** SERVING TIP

If scallions are not available, use chopped chives or parsley.

 STOVETOP

# CURRIED SHRIMP SKEWERS WITH CILANTRO

Tender shrimp cooked in peanut oil, curry, garlic, and ginger and served with fresh green cilantro leaves creates an exotic appetizer.

**PREP:** 12 minutes • **COOK:** 5 minutes • **SERVINGS:** 8

## Ingredients

1 pound uncooked large shrimp, peeled, deveined, tails removed

salt and ground black pepper

3 tablespoons peanut oil

2 teaspoons curry powder

2 cloves garlic, minced

1 tablespoon minced fresh ginger

Wooden picks

fresh cilantro leaves

## Directions

**1.** Season shrimp with salt and black pepper.

**2.** Place peanut oil, curry powder, garlic, and ginger into pot. Set to STOVETOP HIGH. Cook uncovered 1 minute or until garlic is tender, stirring often. Stir in shrimp. Cook uncovered 4 minutes or until shrimp are cooked through, stirring occasionally. Serve shrimp on wooden picks with cilantro leaf on top.

## NINJA SERVING TIP

Try another, more spicy version: Replace curry powder with red or green curry paste and cook according to the above directions.

Appetizers

# KOREAN CHICKEN WINGS

The blend of soy sauce, brown sugar, garlic, and ginger doesn't only coat these wings; slow cooking intensifies the flavor and helps permeate the meat, making them delicious through and through.

**PREP:** 10 minutes • **COOK:** 3–5 hours • **SERVINGS:** 4

## Ingredients

**2 pounds chicken wings, tips removed**

**½ cup soy sauce**

**¼ cup packed brown sugar**

**3 cloves garlic, minced**

**2 tablespoons peeled, chopped fresh ginger**

**3 green onions, thinly sliced**

## Directions

**1.** Set pot to STOVETOP HIGH. Add chicken to pot. Cook uncovered 5 minutes or until chicken is lightly browned on both sides.

**2.** Stir soy sauce, brown sugar, garlic, ginger, and green onions in bowl. Pour soy sauce mixture over chicken and toss to coat. Set to SLOW COOK LOW for 3–5 hours. Cover and cook until chicken is cooked through.

**NINJA** SERVING TIP

Double the recipe for a great party dish and keep warm in pot on SLOW COOK WARM.

STOVETOP/OVEN

# KALE- OR SPINACH-STUFFED MUSHROOMS

Kale is one of the healthiest vegetables to add to your regular cooking recipe list. This recipe takes just over the 30-minute limit for 30-minute meals, but the extra 3 minutes will be well worth it.

**PREP:** 10 minutes • **COOK:** 33 minutes • **SERVINGS:** 8–10

## Ingredients

**32 white button, cremini, or baby portabella mushrooms**

**olive oil spray**

**2 cloves garlic, minced**

**5 ounces kale or baby spinach, stemmed (about 3 cups)**

**kosher salt and pepper**

**3 slices turkey bacon, cooked**

**2 ounces low-fat Swiss cheese, grated**

**¾ cup panko bread crumbs**

## Directions

**1.** Set pot to STOVETOP HIGH.

**2.** Remove stems from mushrooms. Lightly coat bottom of pot with olive oil spray. Add garlic and mushroom stems and cook 2–3 minutes until softened, stirring occasionally. Add kale, salt, and pepper and cook 2–3 more minutes until kale is just softened and wilted.

**3.** Remove mixture from pot, and add turkey bacon and Swiss cheese. Place in food processor, and pulse until desired texture.

**4.** Stir in the bread crumbs. Fill mushroom caps with stuffing. Place mushrooms on bottom of pot. Set OVEN to 375°F and bake for 12–15 minutes. Serve warm.

**NINJA** SERVING TIP

You can use a combination of mushrooms for a more complex flavor.

 STOVETOP

# CHILI CHICKEN MANGO SKEWERS

Chicken cooks in only 6 minutes in garlic, jalapeño, and spicy chili sauce. Sweet chunks of mango and fresh cilantro leaves balance the spice in these tempting little appetizers.

**PREP:** 30 minutes • **COOK:** 6 minutes • **SERVINGS:** 10

## Ingredients

1 pound boneless, skinless chicken breast halves, cut into 1-inch pieces

salt and freshly ground black pepper

2 tablespoons canola oil

2 cloves garlic, minced

1 jalapeño pepper, seeded and minced

2 tablespoons sriracha (spicy chili sauce)

3 ripe mangoes, peeled, cut into 1-inch pieces

30 fresh cilantro leaves

30 wooden picks

## Directions

**1.** Season chicken with salt and black pepper.

**2.** Add oil, garlic, and jalapeño pepper to pot. Set to STOVETOP HIGH. Cook uncovered 1 minute or until pepper is tender. Stir in chicken. Cook uncovered 5 minutes or until chicken is cooked through, stirring occasionally. Stir in sriracha. Cook 1 minute. Remove chicken from pot.

**3.** Thread 1 piece mango, 1 leaf cilantro, and 1 piece chicken on each wooden pick.

**NINJA** SERVING TIP

Substitute beef steak, cut into 1-inch strips, for chicken for another great appetizer.

STOVETOP/STEAM OVEN

# CHICKEN & VEGETABLE SKEWERS WITH THAI COCONUT SAUCE

These wonderful little skewers are perfect for dipping and cook at the same time as the dipping sauce itself! Party-ready in no time.

**PREP:** 20 minutes • **COOK:** 15 minutes • **SERVINGS:** 8

## Ingredients

1 lime

24 wooden picks

1 onion, cut into ½-inch pieces

1 pound skinless, boneless chicken breast halves, cut into 1-inch pieces

1 red pepper, cut into ½-inch pieces

salt and ground black pepper

2 tablespoons canola oil

2 cloves garlic, minced

1 piece (1 inch) fresh ginger, peeled and minced

1 teaspoon red curry paste

1 can (13.5 ounces) coconut milk

2 tablespoons cornstarch

2 tablespoons cold water

fresh cilantro leaves

## Directions

**1.** Grate zest and squeeze juice from lime.

**2.** Thread 1 piece onion, 1 piece chicken, and 1 piece red pepper on each wooden pick. Season with salt and black pepper.

**3.** Stir oil, garlic, ginger, and curry paste into pot. Set to STOVETOP HIGH. Cook uncovered 2 minutes or until garlic and ginger are tender, stirring occasionally. Stir in coconut milk and lime zest. Season with salt and black pepper.

**4.** Place skewers on rack. Place rack into pot. Set OVEN to 350°F for 10 minutes. Cover and cook until chicken is cooked through. Remove skewers and rack from pot.

**5.** Stir cornstarch, water, and lime juice in bowl. Stir cornstarch mixture into pot. Set to STOVETOP HIGH. Cook uncovered 2 minutes or until mixture is thickened, stirring constantly. Season with salt and black pepper.

**6.** Serve skewers with coconut sauce. Garnish with cilantro leaves.

**NINJA** SERVING TIP

Toss leftover Thai coconut sauce with cilantro and cooked soba noodles or linguine the next day for lunch.

# CHILI CHEESE CORN MUFFINS

These little flavor-packed muffins add punch to any appetizer platter or even the simplest meal. Consistent heat in the pot helps keep muffins moist and tender.

**PREP:** 10 minutes • **COOK:** 25 minutes • **SERVINGS:** 6

## Ingredients

**cooking spray**

**¾ cup yellow cornmeal**

**¼ cup all-purpose flour**

**1 tablespoon sugar**

**1 teaspoon baking powder**

**½ teaspoon salt**

**1 egg**

**½ cup sour cream**

**¼ cup butter, melted**

**½ cup shredded Cheddar cheese**

**¼ cup corn**

**2 tablespoons chopped canned green chilies**

**2 tablespoons chopped fresh cilantro leaves**

## Directions

1. Spray 6-cup muffin pan with cooking spray. Stir cornmeal, flour, sugar, baking powder, and salt in a bowl. Add egg, sour cream, butter, cheese, corn, chilies, and cilantro and stir until just combined. Spoon batter into muffin-pan cups.

2. Place pan into pot, on rack. Set OVEN to 425°F for 25 minutes. Cover and cook until wooden pick inserted in centers comes out clean. Remove pan from pot. Let muffins cool 5 minutes.

**NINJA** SERVING TIP

Serve with cilantro butter. Stir ¼ cup softened butter with 1 tablespoon cilantro and ¼ teaspoon grated lime zest.

WHITE TURKEY CHILI

# CHAPTER 4:
## Soups/ Stews

STOVETOP/SLOW COOK

# BUTTERNUT SQUASH & APPLE SOUP

This soup tastes decadent but is packed with nutrients and fiber. Using a hand blender or immersion blender for the last step keeps it all in one pot!

**PREP:** 15 minutes • **COOK:** 1 hour, 10 minutes • **SERVINGS:** 6

## Ingredients

**2 tablespoons butter**

**1 package (20 ounces) fresh peeled, cubed butternut squash (about 4 cups)**

**1 large onion, chopped**

**1 large Granny Smith apple, peeled, cored, and chopped**

**¼ teaspoon pumpkin pie spice or ground cinnamon**

**1 teaspoon salt**

**¼ teaspoon ground black pepper**

**3 cups chicken broth**

**2 bay leaves**

**¼ cup half-and-half**

## Directions

**1.** Place butter, squash, onion, and apple into pot. Set to STOVETOP HIGH. Cook uncovered 10 minutes or until squash is lightly browned, stirring occasionally. Stir in pumpkin pie spice, salt, and black pepper.

**2.** Add broth and bay leaves. Set to SLOW COOK HIGH for 1–2 hours. Cover and cook until squash is tender.

**3.** Remove and discard bay leaves. Make sure soup is cooled, then pour soup in batches to blender, making sure the jar is ⅔ full at a time. Puree soup mixture using a blender until smooth. Pour soup back in pot. Stir in half-and-half. Set to STOVETOP HIGH. Cook uncovered 5 minutes or until soup is hot.

### NINJA SERVING TIP

Top each serving with sautéed fresh sage leaves: Heat 1 tablespoon olive oil in skillet over medium-high heat. Add ¼ cup fresh sage leaves. Cook 1 minute, turning once. Carefully remove leaves and drain on paper towels.

STOVETOP/SLOW COOK

# WHITE TURKEY CHILI

Browning turkey and sausage adds an extra dimension of flavor to this wholesome chili — and there's no extra skillet to clean!

**PREP:** 30 minutes • **COOK:** 7–9 hours • **SERVINGS:** 8

## Ingredients

1 can (7 ounces) chipotle peppers in adobo sauce

2 tablespoons olive oil

1 pound ground turkey or chicken

1 pound Italian-style turkey sausage, casing removed

1 small white onion, diced

1 can (4.25 ounces) diced green chiles

2 cans (15.5 ounces each) cannellini beans, drained and rinsed

2½ cups chicken stock

1 clove garlic, chopped

½ teaspoon cayenne pepper

2 tablespoons chili powder

1½ teaspoons ground cumin

½ cup frozen corn

## Directions

**1.** Finely chop half of the chipotle pepper and reserve 1 teaspoon adobo sauce.

**2.** Pour 1 tablespoon oil into pot. Set to STOVETOP HIGH and heat oil. Add turkey to pot. Cook uncovered until turkey is browned, stirring often. Add sausage and remaining oil to pot. Cook uncovered until sausage is browned, stirring often.

**3.** Stir chipotle pepper, reserved adobo sauce, onion, green chiles, beans, stock, garlic, cayenne pepper, chili powder, and cumin into pot. Set to SLOW COOK LOW for 7–9 hours. Cover and cook, stirring in corn during last 30 minutes of cooking time.

**NINJA** SERVING TIP

Top with a lime crema (sour cream and lime juice), diced avocado, diced red or yellow peppers, or cilantro as desired.

**STOVETOP/SLOW COOK**

# GUINNESS BEEF STEW

This traditional Irish dish depends upon the Guinness beer for its memory-invoking flavor; however, any dark beer or stout will make a good substitute.

**PREP:** 5 minutes  •  **COOK:** 2–2½ hours  •  **SERVINGS:** 4

## Ingredients

2 tablespoons flour

1 teaspoon kosher salt

½ teaspoon black pepper

pinch of cayenne

2 pounds stewing beef, trimmed and cut into 1½-inch cubes

3 tablespoons canola or olive oil

2 tablespoons tomato puree

1 12-ounce bottle of Guinness beer

2 large yellow onions, coarsely chopped

2 large garlic cloves, crushed

2 cups carrots, cut into 1-inch-thick pieces

3 sprigs fresh thyme, stemmed

¼ cup minced parsley to garnish

## Directions

1. In a small bowl, combine flour, salt, pepper, and cayenne. In a large bowl, toss meat with 1 tablespoon oil and then sprinkle flour mixture over meat and toss to coat on all sides.

2. Set pot to STOVETOP HIGH and add remaining oil to pot. When oil is hot, add half of meat and brown on all sides. Remove meat and repeat with remaining meat chunks. Add meat back into pot. Reduce heat to STOVETOP LOW. In a small bowl, dissolve tomato puree in ¼ cup Guinness. Stir in onions, garlic, and tomato puree mixture.

3. Cover and cook 5 minutes. Set to STOVETOP HIGH and add half of the remaining beer and bring to a boil. Add the remaining beer, carrots, and thyme. Season to taste. Set to SLOW COOK HIGH for 2 hours, checking for tenderness after 1½ hours (meat and carrots should be fork-tender).

4. Taste and adjust seasonings as desired and garnish with parsley.

 TIME-SAVER TIP

For easy meal prep, start this in the morning and set on SLOW COOKER LOW for 8 hours. Then on SLOW COOK WARM.

STOVETOP/SLOW COOK

# SAUSAGE, CHICKEN, & SHRIMP GUMBO

An important component of making gumbo is the roux, a mixture of flour and oil used to thicken and provide a perfect rich brown color, thanks to the even heat surrounding the pot.

**PREP:** 15 minutes • **COOK:** 7 hours, 30 minutes • **SERVINGS:** 6

## Ingredients

½ cup plus 1 tablespoon vegetable oil

¾ pound smoked sausage, sliced

¾ pound boneless, skinless chicken thighs, cut into 2-inch pieces

⅔ cup flour

1 large onion, chopped

1 medium green pepper, chopped

3 stalks celery, chopped

2 cloves garlic, minced

3 cups chicken broth

1 can (14.5 ounces) diced tomatoes

½ teaspoon dried thyme leaves, crushed

¾ pound uncooked large shrimp, peeled and deveined

## Directions

1. Pour 1 tablespoon oil into pot. Set to STOVETOP HIGH and heat oil. Add sausage and chicken. Cook uncovered 10 minutes or until browned, stirring occasionally. Remove sausage and chicken from pot.

2. Stir in remaining oil and flour. Set to STOVETOP HIGH. Cook uncovered 7 minutes or until flour mixture turns deep brown, stirring constantly with a wooden spoon.

3. Add onion, pepper, celery, and garlic. Cook uncovered 5 minutes or until tender. Stir in broth, tomatoes, and thyme and heat to a boil. Set to SLOW COOK LOW for 7–9 hours. Cover and cook.

4. Stir in shrimp. Set to SLOW COOK HIGH for 15 minutes. Cover and cook until shrimp are cooked through.

**NINJA** SERVING TIP

If you like gumbo with some heat, simply stir in ¼ to ½ teaspoon cayenne pepper with the broth mixture. This recipe is even better when made the day before serving.

STOVETOP/SLOW COOK

# CHICKEN MATZO BALL SOUP

Poaching chicken in the pot keeps texture consistently tender. Turn to SLOW COOK to finish the soup — even the matzo balls, which cook right in the soup!

**PREP:** 20 minutes • **COOK:** 1 hour, 45 minutes • **SERVINGS:** 6

## Ingredients

½ cup matzo meal

2 large eggs

¼ cup vegetable oil or melted butter

2 tablespoons water

1½ teaspoons salt

¾ teaspoon ground black pepper

6 cups chicken broth

1 pound skinless, boneless chicken breast halves

2 carrots, peeled and chopped

1 medium onion, chopped

3 stalks celery, thinly sliced

2 small bay leaves

2 tablespoons chopped fresh parsley

## Directions

1. Stir matzo meal, eggs, oil, water, ½ teaspoon salt, and ½ teaspoon black pepper in bowl. Cover and refrigerate.

2. Pour 1 cup broth into pot and add chicken. Set to STOVETOP HIGH. Cover and cook 15 minutes or until chicken is cooked through. Remove chicken from pot. Using two forks, shred chicken.

3. Add remaining broth, carrots, onion, celery, bay leaves, shredded chicken, and remaining salt and black pepper to pot. Set to SLOW COOK HIGH for 1–2 hours. Cover and cook.

4. Drop rounded tablespoons of matzo mixture into soup. Do not stir. Set to SLOW COOK HIGH for 30 minutes. Cover and cook until matzo balls are cooked through. Sprinkle with parsley.

**NINJA** SERVING TIP

For the perfect main-dish meal, serve with a simple salad. For fluffier matzo balls, try substituting plain seltzer for water.

STOVETOP/SLOW COOK

# CELERY & SWEET POTATO SOUP WITH BARLEY

There's no need to precook the barley in this recipe. It cooks right in the flavorful broth! Chunks of sweet potato and tomato make this vegetarian soup hearty and delicious.

**PREP:** 20 minutes • **COOK:** 4 hours • **SERVINGS:** 6

## Ingredients

1 tablespoon olive oil

4 stalks celery, coarsely chopped

1 large onion, coarsely chopped

3 cloves garlic, minced

2 medium sweet potatoes, peeled and diced

1 teaspoon dried oregano leaves, crushed

½ teaspoon dried basil leaves, crushed

¼ teaspoon ground black pepper

6 cups vegetable broth

1 can (14.5 ounces) diced tomatoes, undrained

½ cup uncooked medium pearl barley

## Directions

**1.** Pour oil into pot. Set to STOVETOP HIGH and heat oil. Add celery and onion to pot. Cook uncovered 10 minutes or until vegetables are tender-crisp, stirring occasionally. Stir in garlic. Cook uncovered 2 minutes, stirring often.

**2.** Stir in potatoes, oregano, basil, black pepper, broth, tomatoes, and barley. Set to SLOW COOK HIGH for 4–5 hours. Cover and cook until barley is tender.

**NINJA** SERVING TIP

For an easy flavor twist, add 1 small head fresh fennel, coarsely chopped, with onion and celery.

STOVETOP/SLOW COOK

# CHILI WITH CORN BREAD CRUST

Spicy red chili with beans simmers in pot, then corn bread batter is spooned on top. The corn bread bakes right on top of the chili — this main dish and side dish in one is perfect for a cold winter night!

**PREP:** 20 minutes • **COOK:** 4 hours, 10 minutes • **SERVINGS:** 6

## Ingredients

**1 tablespoon vegetable oil**

**1½ pounds ground beef or turkey**

**1 large onion, diced**

**1 green pepper, diced**

**1 tablespoon chili powder**

**½ teaspoon ground cinnamon**

**1 can (28 ounces) diced tomatoes, undrained**

**1 can (about 15 ounces) kidney beans, rinsed and drained**

**1 tablespoon tomato paste**

**1 package (8.5 ounces) corn muffin mix**

**1 egg, beaten**

**⅓ cup milk**

## Directions

1. Pour oil into pot. Set to STOVETOP HIGH and heat oil. Add beef, onion, and pepper to pot. Cook uncovered 10 minutes or until beef is browned, stirring occasionally. Spoon off any fat. Add chili powder and cinnamon to pot. Cook 5 minutes, stirring occasionally.

2. Stir tomatoes, beans, and tomato paste in pot. Set to SLOW COOK HIGH for 4–5 hours. Cover and cook.

3. After 4½ hours of cooking time, stir muffin mix, egg, and milk in bowl. Uncover pot and spoon batter over chili. Cover and cook 30 minutes or until corn bread is cooked through.

**NINJA** SERVING TIP

Serve with sour cream and shredded Cheddar cheese.

STOVETOP/SLOW COOK

# CHICKEN TORTILLA SOUP

This flavorful soup yields hearty bowlfuls of shredded chicken, tomatoes, beans, corn, and tortilla strips. Browning the chicken, then slow simmering in the pot, locks in the flavor.

**PREP:** 20 minutes • **COOK:** 2 hours, 5 minutes • **SERVINGS:** 8

## Ingredients

1 tablespoon canola oil

1¼ pounds boneless, skinless chicken breast halves

1 medium onion, chopped

2 cloves garlic, chopped

¼ cup fresh cilantro leaves, chopped

2 cans (14.5 ounces each) diced tomatoes, undrained

2 cans (10 ounces each) enchilada sauce

1 can (14.5 ounces) low-sodium chicken broth

1 can (about 15 ounces) black beans, undrained

1 package (10 ounces) frozen corn, thawed

1 tablespoon each chili powder and ground cumin

5 corn tortillas (6-inch), cut into 3 x ½-inch strips

## Directions

**1.** Pour oil into pot. Set to STOVETOP HIGH and heat oil. Add chicken to pot. Cook uncovered 5 minutes or until chicken is lightly browned on both sides.

**2.** Stir onion, garlic, cilantro, tomatoes, enchilada sauce, broth, beans, corn, chili powder, and cumin in pot. Set to SLOW COOK HIGH for 2–3 hours. Cover and cook until chicken is fork-tender.

**3.** Place chicken in large bowl. Using two forks, shred chicken. Place chicken back in pot with soup. Top soup with tortillas before serving.

**NINJA** SERVING TIP

This soup is delicious served with diced avocado sprinkled on top with the tortillas.

STOVETOP/SLOW COOK

# RED LENTIL & LEMON SOUP

Lentils are a great source of fiber, so this soup is light-tasting but very hearty. The lemon adds a bright Mediterranean touch. Sautéing the aromatics in the pot first brings out their flavor and gives dimension to the soup.

**PREP:** 15 minutes • **COOK:** 5 hours, 10 minutes • **SERVINGS:** 4

## Ingredients

1 tablespoon olive oil

4 medium carrots, peeled and chopped

1 medium onion, chopped

2 cloves garlic, minced

½ teaspoon salt

2 teaspoons ground cumin

1½ cups dried red lentils

6 cups vegetable broth or water

¼ cup lemon juice

## Directions

1. Pour oil into pot. Set to STOVETOP HIGH and heat oil. Add carrots, onion, garlic, and salt to pot. Cook uncovered 5 minutes or until vegetables are tender, stirring occasionally. Stir in cumin.

2. Stir in lentils and broth and heat to a boil. Set to SLOW COOK LOW for 5–7 hours. Cover and cook until lentils are tender. Stir in lemon juice before serving.

**NINJA** HEALTHY TIP

Iron-rich spinach is a beautiful addition to this soup. Stir in 1 package (about 10 ounces) fresh baby spinach. Cook 5 minutes or just until spinach is wilted. Don't overcook or you'll lose the bright green color.

STOVETOP/SLOW COOK

# FRENCH ONION SOUP

Simple ingredients meet to make a sublime version of this classic soup. Onions are caramelized right in the pot, then finished on SLOW COOK in the herb brandy broth until silky.

**PREP:** 10 minutes • **COOK:** 1 hour, 16 minutes • **SERVINGS:** 4

## Ingredients

¼ **cup butter**

**2 large onions, thinly sliced**

**6 sprigs fresh thyme**

1½ **tablespoons chopped fresh rosemary leaves**

**salt and ground black pepper**

¾ **cup brandy**

¼ **cup all-purpose flour**

**1 container (32 ounces) beef stock**

**12 oven-baked garlic Italian toasts**

½ **pound shredded Gruyère cheese**

## Directions

1. Place butter into pot. Set to STOVETOP HIGH. Heat uncovered until butter is melted. Add onions, thyme, rosemary, salt, and black pepper. Cook uncovered 15 minutes or until onions are very tender, stirring occasionally. Stir in brandy and flour. Cook uncovered 1 minute or until mixture is thickened, stirring constantly.

2. Pour stock into pot. Season with salt and black pepper. Set to SLOW COOK HIGH for 1–2 hours. Cover and cook.

3. Place three toasts in each of the four bowls. Sprinkle with cheese. Spoon soup over cheese-topped toasts.

**NINJA** SERVING TIP

If you can't find Italian toasts, use garlic or other purchased croutons.

STOVETOP/SLOW COOK

# CAULIFLOWER SOUP

Sauté cauliflower, make homemade cream sauce, then simmer to perfection, all in one pot! You can make a special soup like this one anytime when it's this easy.

**PREP:** 10 minutes • **COOK:** 2 hours, 20 minutes • **SERVINGS:** 4

## Ingredients

**1 tablespoon olive oil**

**1 head cauliflower (about 1½ pounds), trimmed and cut into florets**

**1 small onion, chopped**

**2 small cloves garlic, minced**

**2 tablespoons butter, melted**

**2 tablespoons all-purpose flour**

**1 teaspoon salt**

**¼ teaspoon ground black pepper**

**¼ teaspoon ground nutmeg**

**1 carton (32 ounces) vegetable broth**

## Directions

**1.** Pour oil into pot. Set to STOVETOP HIGH and heat oil. Add cauliflower, onion, and garlic to pot and toss to coat. Cook uncovered 5 minutes or until cauliflower is browned, stirring occasionally.

**2.** Stir butter, flour, salt, black pepper, and nutmeg into pot. Cook uncovered 2 minutes, stirring constantly. Stir in 2 cups broth. Cover and cook 5 minutes or until mixture boils and thickens. Stir in remaining broth. Set to SLOW COOK HIGH for 2–3 hours. Cover and cook until cauliflower is tender.

**3.** Puree soup mixture using a blender until smooth. Make sure soup is cooled, then pour soup in batches to blender, making sure the jar is ⅔ full at a time. Place soup back into pot. Set to STOVETOP HIGH. Cook uncovered 5 minutes or until soup is hot.

**NINJA** SERVING TIP

Add croutons and a thinly sliced cauliflower floret for a pretty garnish for this soup.

 STOVETOP/SLOW COOK

# HEARTY SEAFOOD STEW

Enjoy the savory slow-cooked broth of tomatoes, wine, fennel, and onion for dipping crusty, warm Italian bread with your meal.

**PREP:** 15 minutes • **COOK:** 4 hours • **SERVINGS:** 6

## Ingredients

2 tablespoons olive oil

1 medium onion, chopped

1 bulb fennel, thinly sliced crosswise

1 clove garlic, chopped

½ teaspoon crushed red pepper

1 cup dry white wine

1 can (14.5 ounces) diced tomatoes, undrained

½ pound large sea scallops

¾ pound cod fillets, cut into 1-inch pieces

½ pound uncooked jumbo shrimp, peeled and deveined

2 pounds mussels, scrubbed

1 loaf crusty Italian bread, sliced and toasted

## Directions

**1.** Add oil, onion, fennel, garlic, and red pepper to pot. Set to STOVETOP HIGH. Cook uncovered 3 minutes or until onions are tender, stirring occasionally.

**2.** Stir in wine and tomatoes. Cover and set to SLOW COOK HIGH for 3–4 hours. After 3½ hours, add seafood and cook 20–30 minutes or until mussels open and seafood is cooked through. Discard mussels that do not open. Serve with bread.

### NINJA SERVING TIP

To toast bread, brush bread slices on both sides with olive oil, season with salt and pepper, and place on baking sheet. Bake at 400°F 10–15 minutes or until golden.

STOVETOP/SLOW COOK

# THAI-STYLE PORK STEW

An inexpensive cut of pork and ingredients from your pantry become a special-occasion dish with very little effort. Choose the time that works best for you — either 4 hours on HIGH or 7 hours on LOW.

**PREP:** 10 minutes • **COOK:** 4 hours, 10 minutes • **SERVINGS:** 6

## Ingredients

**1 boneless pork shoulder roast (2½ to 3 pounds)**

**salt and ground black pepper**

**1 tablespoon vegetable oil**

**2 medium red peppers, cut into 1-inch pieces**

**6 green onions, cut into 1½-inch pieces**

**3 cloves garlic, minced**

**⅛ cup each teriyaki sauce and rice wine vinegar**

**1 tablespoon hot pepper sauce**

**⅓ cup creamy peanut butter**

**hot cooked basmati rice**

**½ cup dry-roasted peanuts**

## Directions

**1.** Season pork with salt and black pepper.

**2.** Pour oil into pot. Set to STOVETOP HIGH and heat oil. Place pork into pot. Cook uncovered 15 minutes or until pork is browned on all sides. Add peppers, half of green onions, garlic, teriyaki sauce, vinegar, and pepper sauce. Set to SLOW COOK HIGH for 4–5 hours. Cover and cook until pork is tender.

**3.** Remove pork to cutting board and cut into 1-inch pieces. Stir peanut butter into pot. Return pork to pot. Serve pork mixture over rice. Sprinkle with remaining onions and peanuts.

**NINJA** SERVING TIP

Toss some chopped fresh parsley into cooked rice.

 STOVETOP

# LENTIL SOUP WITH KALE & PESTO

**Lentils and kale are two superfoods that combine perfectly in this mouthwatering dish.**

**PREP:** 10 minutes • **COOK:** 1 hour • **SERVINGS:** 4

## Ingredients

1½ tablespoons olive oil

1 large carrot, diced in ⅓-inch pieces

1 large parsnip, diced in ⅓-inch pieces

1 large stalk celery, diced in ⅓-inch pieces

1 medium onion, diced

1 small sweet potato, peeled and diced in ⅓-inch pieces

1 cup lentils

4 cups vegetable stock, plus an additional 3 cups water or vegetable stock

1 small bunch kale, stemmed and center rib removed, torn into 2 x 2-inch pieces

kosher salt and pepper

prepared pesto

1 lemon, quartered

## Directions

1. Place olive oil in the pot and set to STOVETOP HIGH. Add carrot, parsnip, celery, onion, and sweet potato to pot. Cook until vegetables are tender, remove, and set aside.

2. Add lentils and 4 cups vegetable stock and bring to a boil. Reduce heat to STOVETOP LOW and cook 20–25 minutes or until lentils are soft but are still holding their shape.

3. Add vegetables back into pot, add additional stock or water, set to STOVETOP HIGH, and bring to a boil.

4. Reduce heat to STOVETOP LOW, and add kale. Cook until kale is wilted and tender. Season with salt and pepper to taste.

**NINJA** SERVING TIP

Also add a garnish of lemon zest for color and to add an extra acidic bite.

STOVETOP/SLOW COOK

# HEARTY BEEF STEW

Why brown and braise the beef in the same pot? You keep all the rich flavor of the browning, and it makes cleanup a breeze. This recipe adds the convenience of the slow cooker — no tending needed!

**PREP:** 10 minutes • **COOK:** 7 hours, 10 minutes • **SERVINGS:** 8

## Ingredients

**2 pounds stewing beef**

**1 teaspoon salt**

**½ teaspoon ground black pepper**

**¼ cup all-purpose flour**

**2 tablespoons vegetable oil**

**1½ cups beef broth**

**4 red potatoes, cut in half**

**2 onions, cut in quarters**

**1 cup baby carrots**

**4 cloves garlic, chopped**

**2 sprigs fresh thyme or 1 teaspoon dried thyme leaves, crushed**

**1 cup frozen peas, thawed**

## Directions

**1.** Season beef with salt and black pepper. Coat with flour.

**2.** Pour oil into pot. Set to STOVETOP HIGH and heat oil. Add beef and cook uncovered 10 minutes or until browned, stirring occasionally.

**3.** Stir broth, potatoes, onions, carrots, garlic, and thyme into pot. Set to SLOW COOK LOW for 7–9 hours. Cover and cook until beef is fork-tender. Stir in peas during last 10 minutes of cooking time.

**NINJA** TIME-SAVER TIP

You can reduce the SLOW COOK step by slow cooking on HIGH for 4 hours.

 STOVETOP

# PASTA & FAGIOLI

Here is a hearty Italian pasta and bean soup that will stick to your ribs. Use Italian bread to sop up the broth.

**PREP:** 20 minutes • **COOK:** 18 minutes • **SERVINGS:** 8–12

## Ingredients

**1 tablespoon olive oil**

**4 medium onions, chopped**

**4 stalks celery, chopped**

**2 tablespoons garlic, minced**

**1 tablespoon dried parsley**

**2 teaspoons Italian seasoning**

**¼ teaspoon crushed red pepper flakes**

**salt to taste**

**3 quarts vegetable broth**

**2 jars (14.5 ounces) fire-roasted diced tomatoes**

**1 pound ditalini pasta, uncooked**

**2 cans (15.5 ounces) cannellini beans, drained**

**½ cup Parmesan cheese**

## Directions

**1.** Set pot to STOVETOP HIGH and add olive oil. Add onion, celery, and garlic and cover and cook 3 minutes, stirring occasionally.

**2.** Add parsley, Italian seasoning, red pepper flakes, salt, broth, tomatoes, and pasta and stir. Cover and cook 10–12 minutes.

**3.** Add beans, stirring well to incorporate. Cover and cook 4 minutes.

**4.** Garnish with Parmesan cheese and serve immediately.

**NINJA** TIME-SAVER TIP

Turn this soup into the main meal: Add 8 ounces ground beef in step 2 and sauté until meat browns.

**STOVETOP/SLOW COOK**

# CREAMY CORN CHOWDER

Consistent heat from our pot makes from-scratch sauces simple. Add potatoes, corn, and broth and it's hands-free slow cooking to the finish.

**PREP:** 10 minutes • **COOK:** 4 hours, 5 minutes • **SERVINGS:** 6

## Ingredients

2 tablespoons olive oil

1 medium onion, chopped

2 cloves garlic, chopped

8 ounces thick-sliced ham, cut into ¼-inch pieces

3 tablespoons all-purpose flour

1 large unpeeled russet potato, cut into ½-inch pieces

1 package (12 ounces) frozen corn, thawed

4 cups chicken broth

1 cup heavy cream

oyster crackers

## Directions

1. Place oil, onion, garlic, and ham in pot. Set to STOVETOP HIGH. Cook uncovered 3 minutes or until onion is tender, stirring occasionally. Stir in flour. Cook uncovered 1 minute, stirring constantly.

2. Add potato, corn, and broth to pot. Set to SLOW COOK HIGH for 4–5 hours. Cover and cook until potato is tender. Stir in cream and serve with crackers.

**NINJA** TIME-SAVER TIP

Substitute 8 ounces chopped, cooked bacon for ham.

103

STOVETOP

# SILKY WINTER CHESTNUT SOUP

Chestnuts contain fewer calories than walnuts and almonds
with no cholesterol and little fat. Plus, this recipe is gluten-free!

**PREP:** 10 minutes • **COOK:** 1 hour • **SERVINGS:** 6–8

## Ingredients

**3 tablespoons unsalted butter**

**½ cup finely chopped celery**

**½ cup finely chopped carrot**

**½ cup finely chopped onion**

**3 fresh flat-leaf parsley sprigs**

**2 whole cloves**

**1 Turkish or ½ California bay leaf**

**6 cups vegetable broth**

**1 jar (14 to 15 ounces) peeled
roasted whole chestnuts, crumbled**

**¼ cup Madeira**

**¼ teaspoon black pepper**

**salt**

**1 cup crème fraîche thinned with a
little heavy cream for drizzling**

## Directions

**1.** Set pot to STOVETOP HIGH. Melt butter and add carrot, celery, and onion. Set to STOVETOP LOW. Cover the pot with lid, then sweat the vegetables 15 minutes until softened.

**2.** Wrap parsley, cloves, and bay leaf in cheesecloth and tie into a bundle with string.

**3.** Add broth and herb bundle to vegetables. Set pot to STOVETOP HIGH and bring liquid to a boil. Reduce heat to STOVETOP LOW and simmer 20 minutes.

**4.** Add the chestnuts and Madeira wine and simmer covered for 3 minutes. Discard herb bundle and let soup cool completely.

**5.** Pour half of the soup into a blender, cover, and blend until smooth. Repeat with the remaining soup.

**6.** Pour pureed soup into pot and set to STOVETOP HIGH. Bring soup to a simmer. Season with salt and pepper and garnish individual bowls with thinned crème fraîche.

## NINJA SERVING TIP

At Christmas, for a change of pace, serve the soup in small demitasse cups as a mini appetizer or hors d'oeuvres.

 STOVETOP

# CHICKEN & DUMPLINGS SOUP

**Dropped or rolled dumplings — it all depends on where you are from. Dropped is easier, and Bisquick makes it well ... quick.**

**PREP:** 20 minutes • **COOK:** 40–45 minutes • **SERVINGS:** 4–6

## Ingredients

**1 rotisserie chicken, pulled or shredded**

**2 quarts chicken stock**

**1 medium onion, diced**

**2 carrots, chopped**

**2 stalks celery, chopped**

**2 cups Bisquick**

**¾ cup milk**

**½ teaspoon salt**

**¼ teaspoon pepper**

**1 tablespoon minced parsley**

## Directions

**1.** Set pot to STOVETOP HIGH. Add stock, onion, carrots, and celery. Cover with lid and cook 15–20 minutes.

**2.** Add chicken, cover, and bring to a boil.

**3.** Meanwhile, in a large bowl, use a fork to stir together the Bisquick, milk, salt, pepper, and parsley, and let rest 10 minutes.

**4.** Set pot to STOVETOP LOW.

**5.** Using two spoons, drop biscuits one at a time into the simmering liquid, cover, and cook 15 minutes. Serve immediately.

**NINJA** SERVING TIP

Try other mix-ins with your biscuits, such as fresh thyme, rosemary, or sage.

**STOVETOP/SLOW COOK**

# CHICKEN SOUP WITH BARLEY & SPINACH

Fresh good-for-you vegetables added to rotisserie chicken, seasoned broth, and barley make for hearty homemade goodness.

**PREP:** 20 minutes • **COOK:** 2 hours, 10 minutes • **SERVINGS:** 8

## Ingredients

2 tablespoons olive or vegetable oil

2 carrots, peeled and chopped

2 cups sliced assorted mushrooms

1 large onion, chopped

2 stalks celery, thinly sliced

1 teaspoon salt

½ teaspoon ground black pepper

6 cups chicken broth

1 cup uncooked pearl barley

2 small bay leaves

1 can (14.5 ounces) diced tomatoes, undrained

1 bag (6 ounces) fresh baby spinach

1 rotisserie chicken, removed from bone and shredded

## Directions

**1.** Add oil, carrots, mushrooms, onion, and celery to pot. Set to STOVETOP HIGH. Cook uncovered 10 minutes or until vegetables are lightly browned, stirring occasionally. Season with salt and black pepper.

**2.** Stir in broth, barley, and bay leaves. Set to SLOW COOK HIGH for 2–3 hours. Cover and cook, stirring in tomatoes, spinach and chicken for last 30 minutes of cooking time. Remove and discard bay leaves before serving.

**NINJA** HEALTHY TIP

This soup makes a terrific dinner. Serve with melon slices and crusty French bread.

**STOVETOP/SLOW COOK**

# BLACK BEAN CHILI

This chili can be meatless or can be custom-made to suit your taste by choosing ground beef, chicken, turkey, or bison.

**PREP:** 10 minutes • **COOK:** 2 hours, 20 minutes • **SERVINGS:** 6

## Ingredients

1 pound ground beef, chicken, or bison (optional)

1 medium onion, chopped

1 large green pepper, chopped

3 cloves garlic

3 jalapeños, stemmed (add in ribs and seeds if you want very hot; otherwise, remove ribs and seeds)

1–2 canned chipotles plus 1 tablespoon adobo sauce

1½ tablespoons ground cumin

2 tablespoons chili powder

1½ teaspoons salt

1 can (28 ounces) crushed tomatoes

2 cans (15-ounces each) black beans

fresh stemmed and chopped cilantro to garnish

## Directions

1. Place meat, onion, pepper, garlic, and jalapeños into pot. Set to STOVETOP HIGH. Cook uncovered 20 minutes or until meat is cooked through, stirring occasionally.

2. Stir in remaining ingredients (except cilantro). Set to SLOW COOK HIGH for 2½–3 hours. Cover and cook. Garnish individual bowls with cilantro.

3. Serve with whole-grain chips and other toppings as desired.

**NINJA** SERVING TIP

Stir in 1 tablespoon of balsamic vinegar to add a sweet and tangy flavor.

**CANTONESE STEAMED CHICKEN**

# CHAPTER 5:
# Steamed Dishes

 STEAMER

# ITALIAN GREEN BEANS

Fresh green beans are quickly steamed to lock in flavor and nutrients, then tossed with a flavorful dressing and served warm or chilled.

**PREP:** 10 minutes • **COOK:** 15 minutes • **SERVINGS:** 4

## Ingredients

**1 cup water**

**1 pound fresh green beans, trimmed**

**1 tablespoon chopped fresh dill weed or 1 teaspoon dried dill weed**

**1 package (0.6 ounces) zesty Italian salad dressing mix, prepared according to package directions**

## Directions

**1.** Pour water into pot and set dial to STEAMER. Set timer to 10 minutes and wait for beep.

**2.** Meanwhile, place green beans on rack. When beep sounds, carefully place rack into pot and cover, checking after 10 minutes for desired doneness.

**3.** With oven mitts, carefully remove rack from pot.

**4.** Stir dill weed into dressing mix. Prepare dressing according to package. Add ⅓ cup dressing mixture and toss to coat. Reserve remaining dressing for another use.

**NINJA** SERVING TIP

The beans can be served at room temperature or chilled. Try adding toasted almonds for a nice crunch.

 **STEAMER**

# MAHIMAHI WITH CITRUS SAUCE

This delicious dish is steamed with the infusions of soy and citrus to create both a tasty entree and a delicious sauce at the same time!

**PREP:** 5 minutes • **COOK:** 8–10 minutes • **SERVINGS:** 4

## Ingredients

1 cup water

1 tablespoon olive oil

1 cup white wine

½ cup orange juice

2 tablespoons soy sauce

1 tablespoon lime juice

4 4-ounce mahimahi fillets

salt and pepper to taste

4 teaspoons Chinese five-spice powder

1 teaspoon sesame seed

2 teaspoons butter

## Directions

1. Add water, olive oil, white wine, orange juice, soy sauce, and lime juice to pot. Set dial to STEAMER. Set timer to 10 minutes.

2. Meanwhile, season each fillet with salt and pepper, five-spice, and sesame seeds.

3. When beep sounds, use oven mitts to carefully place rack into pot and cover, checking after 8–10 minutes for desired doneness.

4. With oven mitts, carefully remove rack from pot.

5. Whisk butter into the sauce at bottom of pot.

6. Divide sauce among plates and top with the fish.

**NINJA** HEALTHY TIP

Add 4 cups of baby spinach to the sauce after you add the butter, stir to wilt then top the fish with the sauce and wilted spinach.

 **STEAMER**

# TILAPIA TACOS

Mexican oregano is stronger than traditional oregano and holds up better with the spices found in most Mexican dishes.

**PREP:** 10 minutes • **COOK:** 7 minutes • **SERVINGS:** 4

## Ingredients

⅛ **teaspoon cumin**

⅛ **teaspoon ground coriander seed**

⅛ **teaspoon Mexican oregano**

**salt and pepper to taste**

**4 4-ounce tilapia fillets**

**2 cups water**

¼ **cup scallion, sliced thin**

½ **cup shredded lettuce**

**4 soft tortilla shells**

¼ **cup salsa**

## Directions

1. Pour water into pot and set dial to STEAMER. Set timer to 7 minutes (cook time) and wait for beep (approximately 7 minutes) to inform you that water is boiling.

2. Meanwhile, mix together cumin, coriander seed, oregano, salt, and pepper. Season tilapia with spice mix and place on rack.

3. When beep sounds, use oven mitts to carefully place rack with fish into pot and place cover on pot.

4. Use oven mitts to carefully remove fish when desired doneness is reached (second beep will sound after cooking preset steaming time is completed).

5. Divide shredded lettuce and sliced tilapia among tortilla shells. Top each with 1 tablespoon salsa, fold over tortilla shells, and serve immediately.

 HEALTHY TIP

Add slices of avocado and tomato to the tacos for a heart-healthy meal.

 STEAMER

# ASPARAGUS WITH LEMON AIOLI

**Asparagus stays beautifully green and fresh — tasting even better after cooking to tenderness. The secret is the steam! A lemony garlic sauce highlights its delicate flavor.**

**PREP:** 10 minutes • **COOK:** 10 minutes • **SERVINGS:** 4

## Ingredients

**1 lemon**

**⅓ cup light mayonnaise**

**1 small garlic clove, minced**

**¼ teaspoon salt**

**ground black pepper**

**1 cup water**

**1 pound asparagus, trimmed**

## Directions

**1.** Pour water into pot, cover, and set dial to STEAMER. Set timer to 10 minutes (cook time) and wait for the beep (approximately 7 minutes) to inform you that water is boiling.

**2.** Meanwhile, for the lemon aioli, grate ½ teaspoon zest and squeeze 2 teaspoons juice from lemon into bowl. Stir in mayonnaise, garlic, and salt. Season with black pepper.

**3.** Place asparagus onto rack.

**4.** When beep sounds, use oven mitts to carefully place rack with asparagus into pot and place cover on pot.

**5.** Use oven mitts to carefully remove rack with asparagus when desired doneness is reached (second beep will sound after preset steaming time is completed).

**6.** Season asparagus with additional salt and black pepper. Serve with lemon aioli.

**NINJA** TIME-SAVER TIP

Some stores carry pre trimmed, washed fresh asparagus in the produce section. Try it to save on prep time!

 **STEAMER**

# CORN ON THE COB

Steaming corn in the husk allows the kernels to cook without overabsorption of water, so your corn will have more flavor than ever before.

**PREP:** 5 minutes • **COOK:** 10–12 minutes • **SERVINGS:** 4

## Ingredients

**1 cups water**

**4 ears corn on the cob**

**4 tablespoons boursin cheese**

**salt and pepper to taste**

## Directions

**1.** Pour water into pot, cover, and set dial to STEAMER. Set timer to 6 minutes (cook time) and wait for the beep (approximately 7 minutes) to inform you that water is boiling.

**2.** Meanwhile pull back the husks on the corn, remove the silk, and then return husks.

**3.** Place corn on the rack. When beep sounds, use oven mitts to carefully place rack with corn into pot and place cover on pot.

**4.** When beep sounds, use oven mitts to carefully remove rack with corn.

**5.** Pull back husk and slather each ear with 1 tablespoon of boursin cheese, season with salt and pepper, replace husk, and serve immediately.

**NINJA** SERVING TIP

For a lower calorie version, substitute your favorite season blend; Italian, Mexican, barbecue etc.

 **STEAMER**

# ASIAN STEAMED VEGETABLES

**Broccoli and cauliflower are both excellent sources of vitamin C and fiber.**

**PREP:** 10 minutes • **COOK:** 6–8 minutes • **SERVINGS:** 4

## Ingredients

¼ **cup teriyaki sauce**

¼ **cup water**

¾ **cup orange juice**

1 **tablespoon sesame oil**

1 **tablespoon Dijon mustard**

¼ **teaspoon pepper**

¼ **teaspoon minced ginger**

1 **teaspoon minced shallots**

10 **ounces broccoli florets**

10 **ounces cauliflower florets**

4 **ounces sliced mushrooms**

## Directions

1. Whisk together teriyaki, water, orange juice, sesame oil, mustard, pepper, ginger, and shallots. Pour mixture into pot, cover, and set dial to STEAMER. Set timer to 8 minutes (cook time) and wait for the beep (approximately 7 minutes) to inform you that water is boiling.

2. Place broccoli, cauliflower, and mushrooms onto rack. When beep sounds, use oven mitts to carefully place rack with vegetables into pot and place cover on pot.

3. Use oven mitts to carefully remove rack with vegetables when desired doneness is reached (second beep will sound after preset steaming time is completed).

4. Serve immediately, topping with steaming liquid if you like.

**NINJA** SERVING TIP

Experiment with different mushrooms (shitake, oyster, cremini, chanterelles, etc.), to give yourself an ever-changing dish.

STOVETOP/STEAMER

# HONEY ORANGE GLAZED CARROTS

These carrots are so delicious, you will want to make them often — thank goodness they're so quick and easy! Carrot slices cook until tender in a glaze of orange, butter, honey, and thyme.

**PREP:** 10 minutes • **COOK:** 18 minutes • **SERVINGS:** 6

## Ingredients

**1 cup water**

**2 large oranges**

**1½ pounds carrots, peeled and cut into ½-inch-thick slices**

**2 tablespoons butter**

**1 teaspoon salt**

**2 tablespoons honey**

**1 teaspoon fresh thyme leaves, minced, or ¼ teaspoon dried thyme**

## Directions

**1.** Grate an orange with zester until ½ teaspoon is collected. Squeeze oranges to collect approximately ¾ cup juice.

**2.** Pour water and orange juice into pot, cover, and set dial to STEAMER. Set timer to 10 minutes (cook time) and wait for the beep (approximately 7 minutes) to inform you that juice is boiling.

**3.** Place carrots onto rack. When beep sounds, use oven mitts to carefully place rack with carrots into pot and place cover on pot.

**4.** When second beep sounds, use oven mitts to move carrots from rack into bottom of pot.

**5.** Add butter and salt to carrots. Set to STOVETOP HIGH until any remaining juice is reduced to 2 tablespoons. Add honey, orange zest and thyme.

**6.** Set to STOVETOP LOW and cook uncovered for 3 minutes, or until carrots are tender, stirring often.

**NINJA** SERVING TIP

These are wonderful served with rotisserie chicken breast and coleslaw purchased at the grocery store.

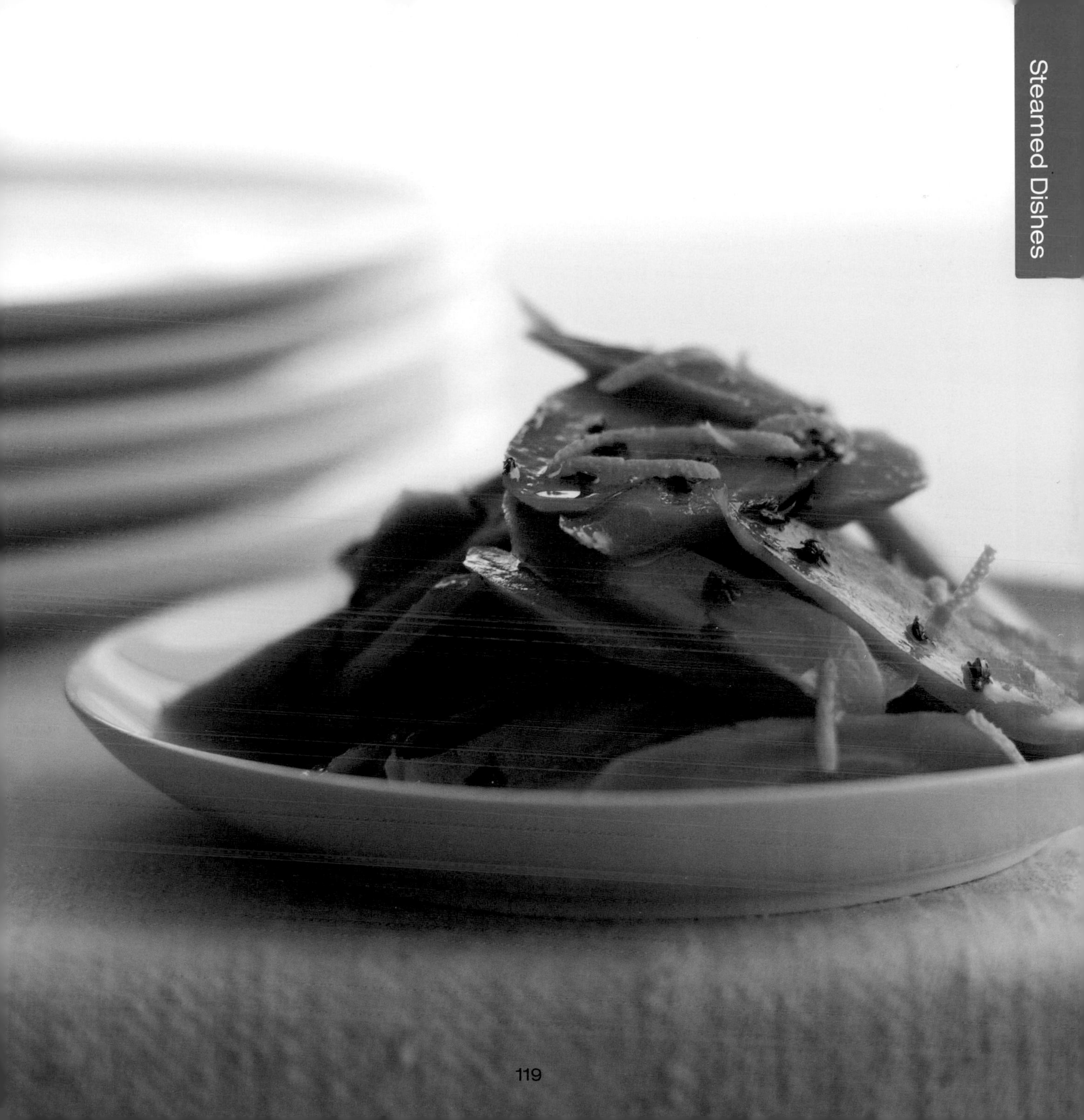

STOVETOP/STEAMER

# GARLIC LEMON STEAMED CLAMS

Onion, garlic, lemon, and beer create a cooking liquid to infuse clams with flavor as they steam. Serve as an appetizer or even a simple meal.

**PREP:** 5 minutes • **COOK:** 20 minutes • **SERVINGS:** 4

## Ingredients

**2 tablespoons olive oil**

**1 small onion, chopped**

**¼ teaspoon salt**

**3 cloves garlic, minced**

**1 cup beer**

**1 lemon, sliced**

**2 tablespoons fresh chopped parsley**

**2 dozen clams, scrubbed**

## Directions

**1.** Pour oil into pot. Set to STOVETOP HIGH and heat oil. Add onion and salt to pot. Cook uncovered 6 minutes or until onions are tender, stirring occasionally. Add garlic. Cook uncovered 1 minute, stirring often.

**2.** Add beer, lemon, and parsley to pot and cover. Set dial to STEAMER and timer to 10 minutes (cook time). Wait for the beep (approximately 7 minutes) to inform you that water is boiling.

**3.** Meanwhile, place clams on rack. When beep sounds, use oven mitts to carefully place rack with clams into pot and place cover on pot.

**4.** Cook until clams open. Use oven mitts to carefully remove rack with clams from pot. Serve clams with broth mixture.

**NINJA** SERVING TIP

Serve this dish with crusty bread for soaking up all the delicious broth.

STEAMER

# MUSSELS FRA DIAVOLO

**Fra Diavolo translates to Devil's Sauce, which is a reference to its spicy nature.**

**PREP:** 5 minutes • **COOK:** 7 minutes • **SERVINGS:** 4

## Ingredients

**2 cups Fra Diavolo sauce**

**1 cup water**

**1 pound mussels, cleaned and debearded**

**3 long hot peppers, sliced into rings**

## Directions

**1.** Add Fra Diavolo sauce and water into pot, cover, and set dial to STEAMER. Set timer to 7 minutes (cook time) and wait for the beep (approximately 10 minutes) to inform you that water is boiling.

**2.** Meanwhile, place mussels on rack and top with pepper slices. When beep sounds, use oven mitts to carefully place rack with mussels into pot and place cover on pot.

**3.** When mussels are done, use oven mitts to carefully remove rack with mussels (second beep will sound after preset steaming time is completed).

**4.** Split sauce from pot among four bowls and place mussels and peppers on top of sauce.

**NINJA** SERVING TIP

Wonderful served over pasta, just add 1 more cup of water and 8 ounces of your favorite pasta, then cook for an additional 9-12 minutes, depending on the pasta.

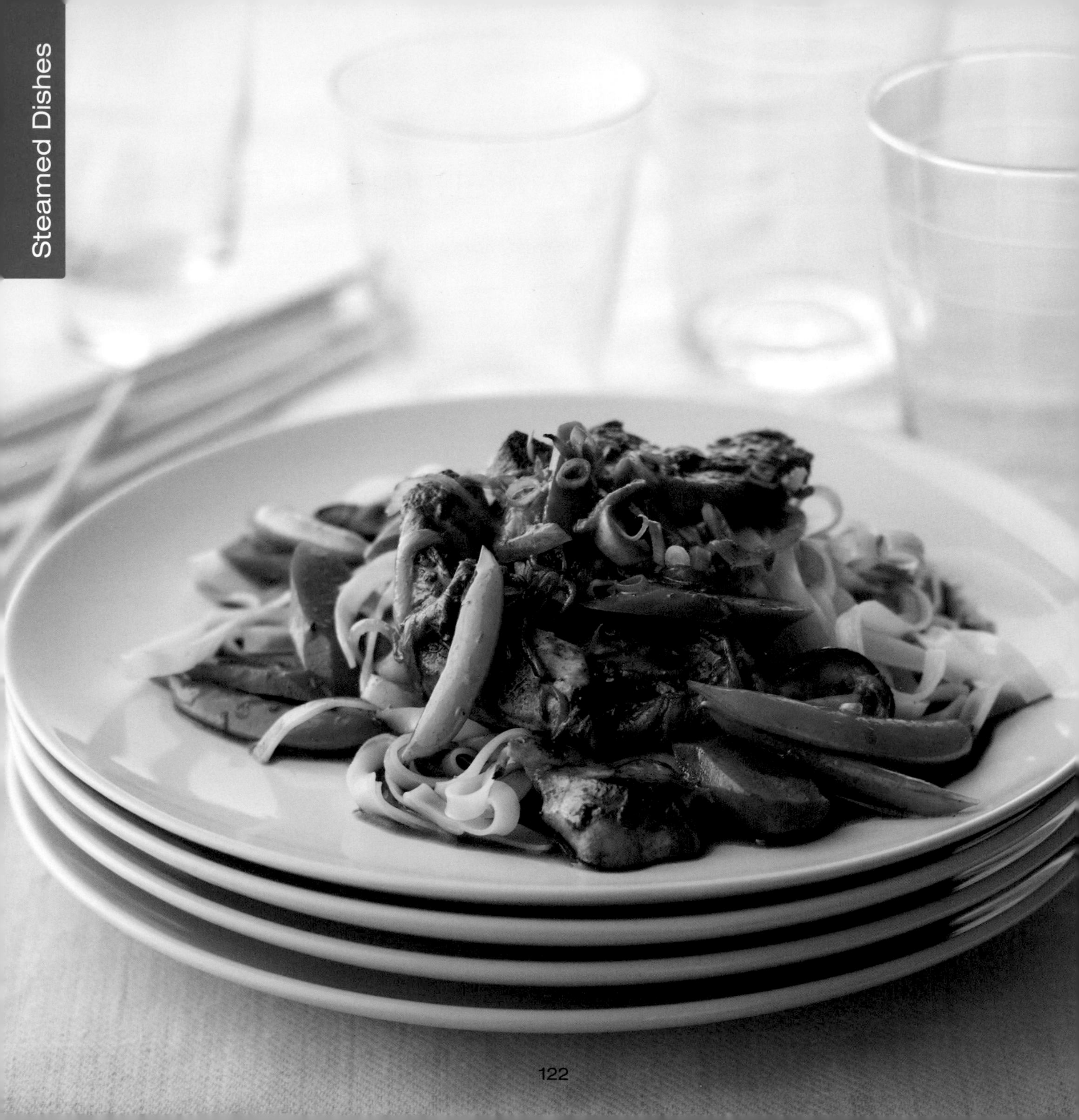

**STOVETOP/STEAMER**

# CANTONESE STEAMED CHICKEN

Steaming the chicken results in a wonderfully tender texture that's infused with the flavors of soy sauce, honey, and ginger. The vegetables and sauce cook in the bottom of the pot and create that delicious-scented steam.

**PREP:** 5 minutes • **COOK:** 25 minutes • **SERVINGS:** 4

## Ingredients

**2 tablespoons soy sauce**

**1 tablespoon rice wine vinegar**

**1 tablespoon minced fresh ginger**

**1 tablespoon honey**

**¼ teaspoon crushed red pepper**

**4 thin-sliced chicken breasts (about 1 pound)**

**1 tablespoon vegetable oil**

**1 medium onion, sliced**

**2 carrots, sliced ¼-inch thick**

**½ cup chicken broth**

**8 ounces sugar snap peas, strings removed**

**6 shiitake mushrooms, stemmed and sliced**

### NINJA SERVING TIP

Serve the chicken and vegetable mixture over hot cooked rice or noodles and sprinkle with sliced fresh chives.

## Directions

**1.** Stir soy sauce, vinegar, ginger, honey, and crushed red pepper in bowl. Add chicken and toss to coat.

**2.** Pour oil into pot. Set to STOVETOP HIGH and heat oil. Add onions and carrots and cook uncovered 7 minutes, stirring occasionally.

**3.** Remove chicken from soy sauce mixture and place on rack.

**4.** Pour soy sauce mixture and chicken broth into pot with onions and carrots. Set dial to STEAMER. Set timer to 12 minutes (cook time) and wait for the beep (approximately 7 minutes) to inform you that water is boiling.

**5.** When beep sounds, use oven mitts to carefully place rack with chicken into pot and place cover on pot. Steam 5 minutes. Remove cover, add sugar snap peas and mushrooms, and cook another 7 minutes until chicken is cooked through and vegetables are just tender.

**6.** Use oven mitts to carefully remove chicken when desired temperature is reached (second beep will sound after preset steaming time is completed).

 **STEAMER**

# EASY STEAMED ARTICHOKES

There are dozens of ways to serve artichoke, both the leaves and the bottom. This is the quick and easy way to have Artichokes perfectly steamed in just 20 minutes.

**PREP:** 5 minutes • **COOK:** 20 minutes • **SERVINGS:** 6

## Ingredients

**4 cups water**

**6 artichokes**

**1 lemon cut in half**

**2 tablespoons olive oil**

**fresh chopped parsley**

**coarse sea or kosher salt**

## Directions

1. Pour water into pot and set dial to STEAMER. Set timer to 20 minutes and wait for beep.

2. Meanwhile, trim the artichokes. Pull off any damaged or brown leaves and discard. Using a serrated knife, trim the stems, leaving about half an inch, then cut off the pointy top third of the artichoke.

3. Place the artichokes stem-end up in the rack. When beep sounds, use oven mitts to carefully place rack into the pot and cover, checking after 20 minutes for desired tenderness. If the leaves come off easily and the knife slips easily into the base, the artichokes are ready. If they're not, set steamer for another 10 minutes and check until done.

4. With oven mitts, carefully remove rack from pot. Use tongs to turn artichoke over on serving plate. Squeeze lemon over the leaves, drizzle with olive oil and sprinkle with chopped parsley.

### NINJA SERVING TIP

After eating leaves, when you get to the center of the artichoke, remove the remaining tiny leaves with your hands, and use a large spoon to scoop out the fuzzy hairs in the center of the heart. Cut the heart into 6-8 pieces. Drizzle with lemon and oil.

 STEAMER

# SHRIMP WITH SNAP PEAS & MINT

**The addition of mint is both familiar and unexpected enough to lift this tasty simple dish to the next level.**

**PREP:** 10 minutes • **COOK:** 8–10 minutes • **SERVINGS:** 4

## Ingredients

**2 cups white wine**

**1 clove garlic, minced**

**2 tablespoons butter**

**1 pound shrimp (16–20, peeled and deveined)**

**½ pound sugar snap peas**

**2 tablespoons chopped fresh mint**

**salt and pepper to taste**

## Directions

**1.** Pour wine, garlic, and butter into pot, cover, and set dial to STEAMER. Set timer to 10 minutes (cook time) and wait for the beep (approximately 7 minutes) to inform you that the water is boiling.

**2.** Meanwhile, place shrimp and snap peas on rack, sprinkle with mint, and season with salt and pepper.

**3.** When beep sounds, use cooking its to carefully place rack with shrimp and peas into pot and place cover on pot.

**4.** Use oven mitts to carefully remove fish when desired doneness is reached (second beep will sound after preset steaming time is completed).

**NINJA** SERVING TIP

Continue cooking the liquid used for steaming to reduce into an intense sauce.

PRIME RIB AU JUS

# CHAPTER 6:
## Entrées

# BALSAMIC GLAZED CHICKEN WITH RADICCHIO

Cooking the radicchio enhances its slightly bitter flavor, which balances beautifully with this savory sauce. Browning the chicken in the pot first is essential to creating a rich flavor base — and the radicchio cooks in the same pot, so no extra saucepans to clean.

**PREP:** 10 minutes • **COOK:** 50 minutes • **SERVINGS:** 4

## Ingredients

2 cloves garlic, minced

4 tablespoons chopped fresh rosemary leaves

salt and ground black pepper

4 tablespoons olive oil

4 bone-in chicken breasts (about 2 pounds)

1 large red onion, thickly sliced

¾ cup red wine

½ cup balsamic vinegar

¼ cup water

2 heads radicchio, cut in quarters, keeping stem intact

## Directions

1. Stir garlic, rosemary, salt, black pepper, and 3 tablespoons olive oil in bowl. Rub chicken with garlic mixture. Let stand 20 minutes.

2. Place chicken into pot, skin side down. Set to STOVETOP HIGH. Cook uncovered 5 minutes or until browned. Remove chicken from pot.

3. Add onion to pot. Place rack into pot and place chicken on rack. Pour wine, vinegar, and water over chicken. Set OVEN to 375°F for 40 minutes. Cover and cook until chicken is cooked through.

4. Remove chicken from pot, cover, and keep warm. Add radicchio to onion mixture. Cover and cook 4 minutes or until radicchio is tender. Serve sauce and radicchio over chicken.

**NINJA** SERVING TIP

Serve with smashed potatoes or crusty bread to soak up the delicious sauce.

 **STEAM OVEN**

# PROVENCE CHICKEN

Chicken is rubbed with a flavorful mixture of herbs, garlic, shallot, and Dijon mustard, then browned in the pot to seal in the juices. Steam roasting to finish keeps meat moist and tender.

**PREP:** 10 minutes • **COOK:** 1 hour, 15 minutes • **SERVINGS:** 6

## Ingredients

1 small bunch fresh parsley, chopped

2 garlic cloves, coarsely chopped

1 large shallot, coarsely chopped

1 tablespoon herbes de Provence

1 sprig fresh rosemary, stem removed

1½ tablespoons Dijon-style mustard

1 teaspoon kosher salt

1 teaspoon ground black pepper

3 tablespoons olive oil

grated zest of 1 lemon

6-pound whole roasting chicken, giblets and neck removed

4 cups water or chicken broth

## Directions

**1.** Add parsley, garlic, shallot, herbes de Provence, rosemary, mustard, salt, and black pepper to food processor. Cover and pulse until mixture is finely chopped. With processor running, slowly add 3 tablespoons olive oil. Continue processing until smooth paste forms. Add lemon zest and pulse.

**2.** Rub parsley mixture on chicken, on all sides, under skin, and inside cavity. Set to STOVETOP HIGH and add chicken to pot. Cook 15 minutes or until chicken is browned on all sides. Remove chicken from pot.

**3.** Pour water into pot. Place chicken on rack and place rack into pot. Set OVEN to 350°F for 1 hour, 15 minutes. Cover and cook until chicken is cooked through.

**NINJA** SERVING TIP

Serve with mashed potatoes and oven-browned carrots.

# ROAST BEEF WITH GARLIC MUSTARD CRUST

*Signature*

You won't need a separate skillet and roasting pan to make this restaurant-worthy dish. A crisp, flavorful crust surrounds juicy, tender perfectly cooked beef.

**PREP:** 10 minutes • **COOK:** 1 hour, 5 minutes • **SERVINGS:** 8

## Ingredients

**6 tablespoons butter**

**3 cloves garlic, finely chopped**

**1½ cups panko bread crumbs**

**3 tablespoons finely chopped fresh parsley**

**salt and ground black pepper**

**1 beef eye round roast (2½ to 3 pounds)**

**1½ tablespoons olive oil**

**3 cups beef broth**

**2 tablespoons Dijon-style mustard**

## Directions

**1.** Stir 3 tablespoons butter, garlic, bread crumbs, and parsley in bowl. Season with salt and black pepper.

**2.** Place remaining butter into pot. Set to STOVETOP HIGH and heat until butter is melted. Add bread crumb mixture to pot. Cook uncovered 2 minutes or until bread crumb mixture is lightly browned, stirring occasionally. Remove bread crumb mixture from pot.

**3.** Season beef with salt and black pepper.

**4.** Pour oil into pot. Set to STOVETOP HIGH and heat oil. Add beef to pot. Cook uncovered 15 minutes or until beef is browned on all sides. Remove beef from pot.

**5.** Pour broth into pot. Place rack into pot. Place beef on rack. Set OVEN to 375°F for 45 minutes. Cover and cook 45 minutes for medium-well or until desired doneness.

**6.** Spread mustard on beef and coat with bread crumb mixture.

**NINJA** SERVING TIP

Serve with roasted red potatoes with rosemary.

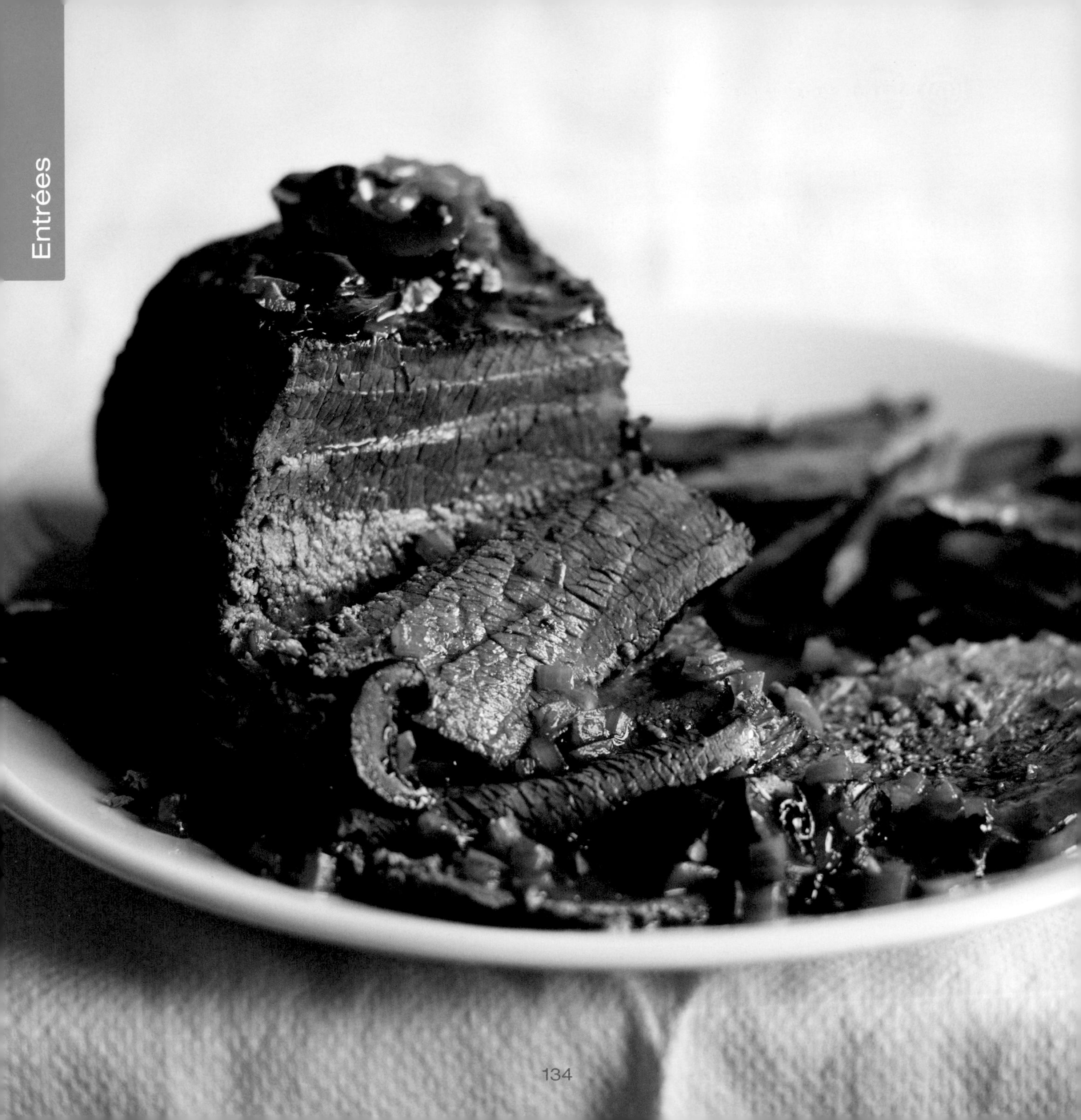

 **STOVETOP/STEAM OVEN**

# COFFEE-BRAISED BEEF WITH MUSHROOM SAUCE

The caramelized flavor from browning the beef in the pot is enhanced by the roasted notes in the coffee. Covered cooking to finish keeps the meat moist and tender.

**PREP:** 10 minutes • **COOK:** 1 hour, 40 minutes • **SERVINGS:** 8

## Ingredients

1 boneless beef rump roast (about 3 pounds)

1 teaspoon salt

½ teaspoon ground black pepper

2 tablespoons butter

2 tablespoons olive oil

1 package (8 ounces) sliced baby Portabella mushrooms

1 large onion, chopped

4 cloves garlic, minced

2 cups strong-brewed black coffee

¼ cup red wine vinegar

¼ cup all-purpose flour

¼ cup cold water

## Directions

1. Season beef with salt and black pepper.

2. Place butter and oil into pot. Set to STOVETOP HIGH and heat until butter is melted. Add beef to pot. Cook uncovered 15 minutes or until beef is browned on all sides. Remove beef from pot.

3. Add mushrooms and onion to pot. Cook uncovered 15 minutes or until vegetables are tender-crisp, stirring occasionally. Stir in garlic. Cook 2 minutes, stirring constantly. Stir in coffee and vinegar.

4. Place beef on rack. Place rack into pot. Set OVEN to 375°F for 55 minutes. Cover and cook 55 minutes for medium or until desired doneness. Remove rack and beef from pot. Cover beef and keep warm.

5. Stir flour and water in bowl until smooth. Stir flour mixture and remaining water into pot. Set to STOVETOP HIGH. Cook uncovered 10 minutes or until mixture boils and thickens, stirring often. Serve beef with mushroom sauce.

**NINJA** HEALTHY TIP

Serve with buttermilk smashed red potatoes and a green salad.

# SWEET & SPICY PORK BABY BACK RIBS

Browning the ribs in the pot seals in the flavor of the smoky-sweet spice rub, then steam roasting cooks the ribs until the meat is falling off the bone. Glazing with barbecue sauce to finish adds an extra layer of flavor.

**PREP:** 10 minutes • **COOK:** 1 hour, 15 minutes • **SERVINGS:** 4

## Ingredients

1 tablespoon smoked paprika

1 tablespoon packed brown sugar

⅛ teaspoon cayenne pepper

1 rack pork baby back ribs (about 3 pounds), cut in half

salt and ground black pepper

1 tablespoon vegetable oil

3 cups beef broth or water

½ cup barbecue sauce

## Directions

1. Stir paprika, brown sugar, and cayenne pepper in bowl. Rub ribs with paprika mixture. Season with salt and black pepper.

2. Pour oil into pot. Set to STOVETOP HIGH and heat oil. Add half the ribs to pot. Cook uncovered 5 minutes or until browned on both sides. Remove ribs from pot. Repeat with remaining ribs. Remove ribs from pot.

3. Pour broth into pot. Place rack into pot. Place ribs on rack. Set OVEN to 375°F for 1 hour. Cover and cook until pork is fork-tender.

4. Uncover pot and brush ribs with sauce. Cook 10 minutes more. Cover and cook until sauce is hot.

**NINJA** SERVING TIP

After cooking, cut ribs in between bones for easy serving.

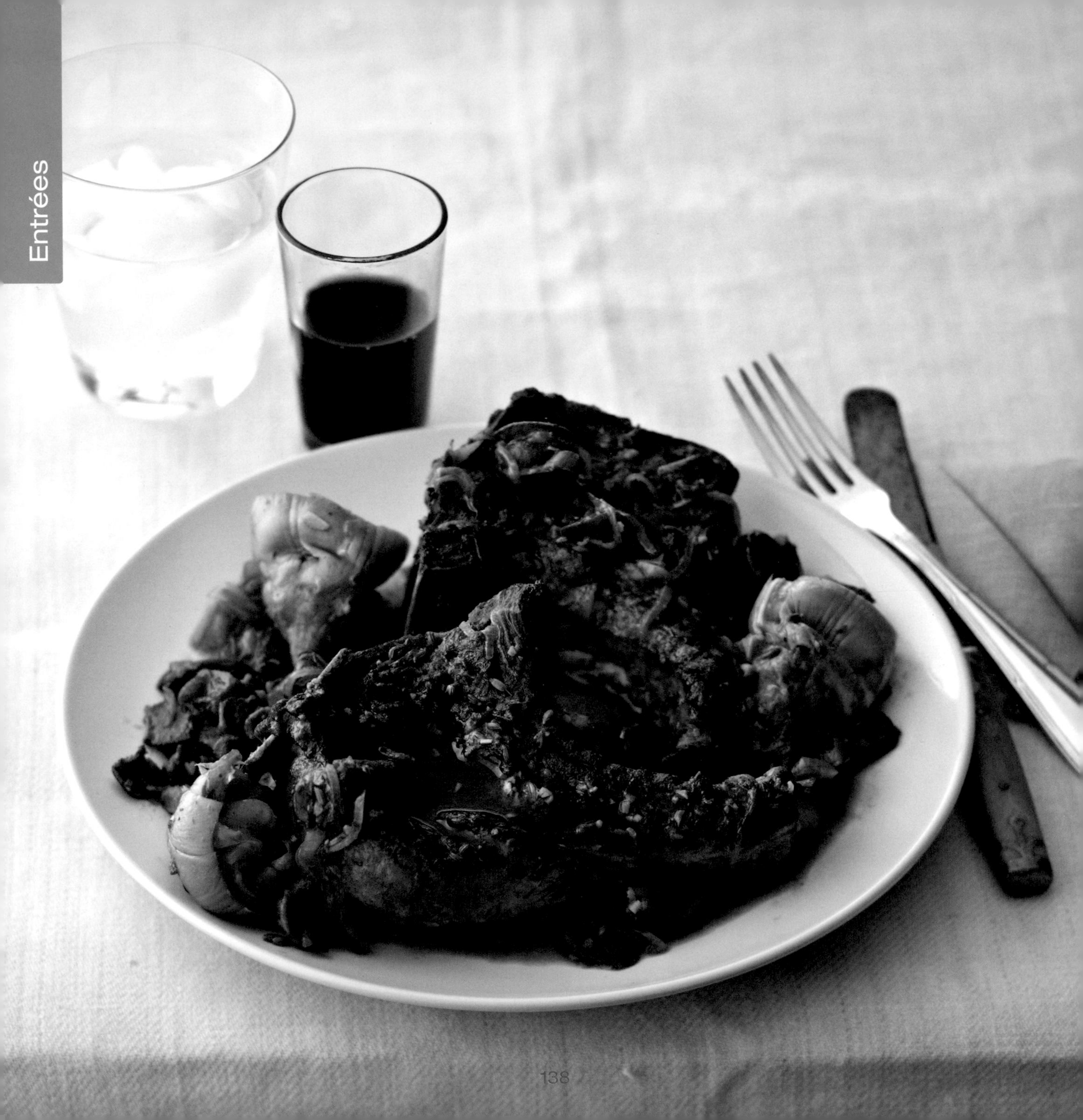

# PORK CHOPS PROVENÇAL

Provençal cooking brings the flavors of France and the Mediterranean together. Pork is simmered in a sauce rich with the flavors of vegetables, bacon, and fennel. Slow cooking melds the flavors for a perfectly seasoned dish.

**PREP:** 15 minutes  •  **COOK:** 5 hours, 25 minutes  •  **SERVINGS:** 6

## Ingredients

¼ **pound bacon, cut into 1-inch strips**

6 **bone-in center-cut pork chops**

**salt and ground black pepper**

1 **large onion, thinly sliced**

3 **cloves garlic, minced**

1 **can (14.5 ounces) chopped tomatoes, undrained**

1 **package (8 ounces) frozen artichoke hearts, thawed and drained**

1 **cup pitted kalamata olives**

1 **tablespoon fennel seeds**

## Directions

1. Set pot to STOVETOP HIGH and place bacon in pot. Cook uncovered 10 minutes or until bacon is crisp, stirring occasionally. Remove bacon from pot and drain on paper towels.

2. Season pork with salt and black pepper. Add pork to pot. Cook 10 minutes or until browned on both sides.

3. Return bacon to pot. Add onion, garlic, tomatoes, artichokes, olives, and fennel seeds to pot. Cook 5 minutes, stirring occasionally. Set to SLOW COOK LOW for 5–7 hours. Cover and cook until pork is fork-tender.

**NINJA** HEALTHY TIP

To provide the same great flavor, substitute turkey bacon for the bacon in this recipe.

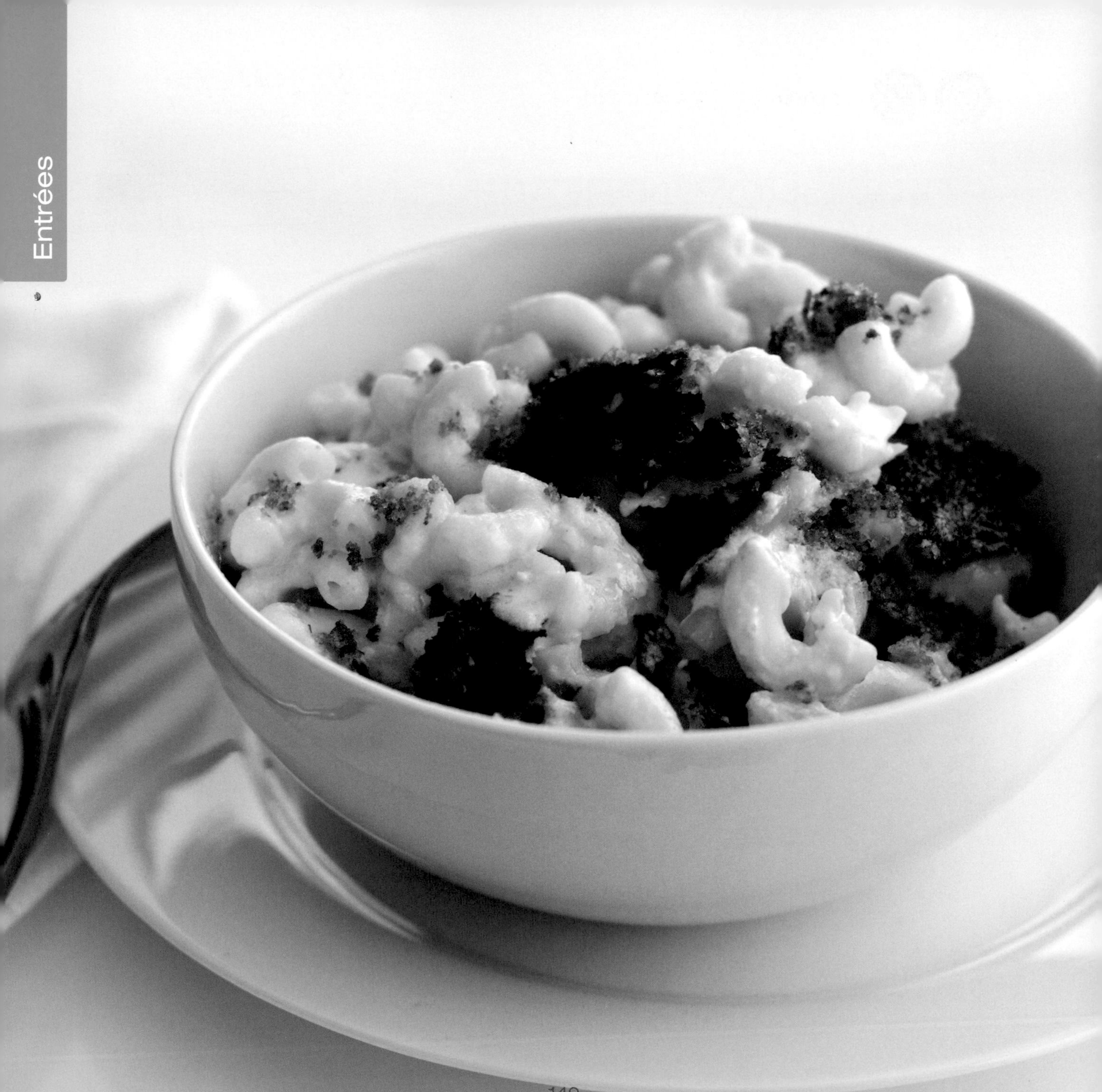

# UPSIDE-DOWN MAC & CHEESE

A macaroni and cheese version of spaghetti pie, this recipe features cheese-sauced pasta baked in a Cheddar bread crumb crust. Everything is cooked in the same pot for easy cleanup.

**PREP:** 15 minutes • **COOK:** 20 minutes • **SERVINGS:** 8

## Ingredients

4 cups water

1 pound uncooked elbow macaroni

¾ cup butter

6 tablespoons all-purpose flour

5 cups whole milk

6¾ cups shredded extra-sharp Cheddar cheese

½ cup grated Pecorino Romano or Parmesan cheese

salt and ground black pepper

cooking spray

1½ cups bread crumbs

## Directions

1. Pour water into pot. Set to STOVETOP HIGH. Heat uncovered to a boil. Stir in macaroni. Cook uncovered 9 minutes or until macaroni is just tender, stirring occasionally. Remove macaroni from pot and drain well in colander, reserving 1 cup cooking water.

2. Add ½ cup butter to pot. Set to STOVETOP LOW and heat until butter is melted. Stir in flour. Cook uncovered 3 minutes, stirring constantly. Add milk and heat to a boil, stirring constantly. Cook uncovered 3 minutes, or until mixture is thickened and smooth, stirring occasionally. Stir in 6 cups Cheddar cheese, ¼ cup Pecorino Romano cheese, salt, and pepper until cheeses are melted, stirring occasionally. Turn off pot.

3. Stir cheese mixture, macaroni, and reserved cooking water in large bowl. Carefully remove pot and wipe dry, allowing it to cool before handling.

4. Melt remaining ¼ cup butter. Stir melted butter, bread crumbs, ¾ cup Cheddar cheese, and ¼ cup Pecorino Romano in bowl.

5. Spray pot with cooking spray. Press bread crumb mixture onto bottom and 1 inch up sides of pot. Pour in macaroni mixture. Set OVEN to 350°F for 20 minutes, checking after 15 minutes. Cook until golden brown on bottom and sides and invert onto plate.

**NINJA** HEALTHY TIP

Serve with sliced fresh tomato salad.

141

**Entrées**

# PRIME RIB AU JUS

Searing the beef in the pot first ensures a flavorful crust that tastes great and helps to seal in the juices. Finish cooking the beef, then use the drippings to create a rich, meaty au jus. A special-occasion main dish, and only one pot to clean!

**PREP:** 10 minutes • **COOK:** 1 hour, 30 minutes • **SERVINGS:** 4

## Ingredients

1 beef standing rib roast (about 5 pounds)

salt and ground black pepper

1 tablespoon chopped fresh rosemary leaves

4 cups beef broth

1 tablespoon butter, softened

1 tablespoon all-purpose flour

## Directions

**1.** Season beef with salt, black pepper, and rosemary. Set pot to STOVETOP HIGH and heat pan. Add beef and cook uncovered 10 minutes or until browned on all sides. Remove beef from pot.

**2.** Pour broth into pot. Place rack into pot. Place beef on rack. Set OVEN to 350°F for 1 hour. Cover and cook 1 hour for medium-rare or until desired doneness. Remove beef to cutting board and cover with foil.

**3.** Stir butter and flour in bowl. Add butter mixture to pot. Set to STOVETOP HIGH. Cook 10 minutes or until mixture is slightly reduced, stirring constantly. Serve sauce with beef.

**NINJA** SERVING TIP

Serve with garlic mashed potatoes and creamed spinach for a real steak house-style dinner!

STOVETOP

# TUSCAN CHICKEN & BEANS

Chicken goes right from the freezer into the pot — no need to thaw!
It cooks until tender in a creamy Italian-seasoned sauce with white
beans and spinach.

**PREP:** 10 minutes  •  **COOK:** 30 minutes  •  **SERVINGS:** 4

## Ingredients

1 tablespoon olive oil

1 medium onion, chopped

2 cloves garlic, chopped

1½ teaspoons Italian seasoning,
   crushed

1 can (14.5 ounces) diced tomatoes,
   undrained

1 can (10.75 ounces) condensed
   cream of chicken soup

1 can (about 15 ounces) cannellini
   beans, rinsed and drained

¼ teaspoon ground black pepper

4 frozen skinless, boneless
   thin-sliced chicken cutlets
   (about 1 pound)

2 cups chopped fresh spinach

## Directions

1. Pour oil into pot. Set to STOVETOP HIGH and heat oil. Add
   onion, garlic, and Italian seasoning to pot. Cook 5 minutes or
   until onion is tender, stirring occasionally.

2. Stir tomatoes, soup, beans, and black pepper into pot and heat
   to a boil. Add frozen chicken to pot. Set to STOVETOP LOW.
   Cover and cook 20 minutes or until chicken is cooked through,
   stirring in spinach during last 5 minutes of cooking time.

**NINJA** SERVING TIP

Sprinkle with Parmesan cheese
before serving.

143

# LEMON CHICKEN WITH ROSEMARY

Fresh lemon and rosemary complement the richly roasted flavor of the chicken, made moist and tender using this foolproof cooking method.

**PREP:** 15 minutes • **COOK:** 1 hour, 15 minutes • **SERVINGS:** 6

## Ingredients

1 lemon

3 sprigs fresh rosemary

6 pound whole roasting chicken

salt and ground black pepper

2 large onions, sliced

3 cloves garlic, sliced

4 cups chicken broth

## Directions

**1.** Grate and reserve 1 tablespoon zest from lemon. Cut lemon in quarters. Chop and reserve 1 sprig rosemary.

**2.** Remove package of giblets and neck from chicken cavities. Rinse chicken and pat dry with paper towel. Place lemon quarters and remaining rosemary sprigs into chicken cavity. Season chicken with salt and pepper.

**3.** Set to STOVETOP HIGH. Place chicken into pot. Cook uncovered, searing chicken for approximately 5–7 minutes on each side as desired. Remove chicken from pot and place on rack.

**4.** Place onions, garlic, and broth into pot. Place rack with chicken in pot. Sprinkle chicken with reserved lemon zest and chopped rosemary. Set OVEN to 375°F for 1 hour and 15 minutes. Cover and cook until chicken is cooked through and juices run clear.

**NINJA** TIME-SAVER TIP

Use leftovers from this delicious chicken for two or more meals later in the week. Great for lunch with mixed salad greens, chopped fresh vegetables, and low-fat dressing.

# SAVORY POT ROAST

This recipe elevates an inexpensive cut of meat to something worthy of a special meal. Browning beef first is essential to creating the rich flavor base, and now you can do it all in the same pot.

**PREP:** 20 minutes • **COOK:** 6–8 hours • **SERVINGS:** 8

## Ingredients

1 boneless beef chuck roast (3 to 4 pounds)

¼ cup plus 2 tablespoons flour

¼ cup olive oil

2 carrots, peeled and chopped

2 stalks celery, chopped

1 medium onion, chopped

3 cloves garlic, crushed

1 can (28 ounces) whole plum tomatoes in purée

1 cup each red wine and beef broth

3 sprigs fresh thyme

2 sprigs fresh rosemary

1 tablespoon butter, softened

## Directions

1. Coat beef with ¼ cup flour.

2. Pour half of oil into pot. Set to STOVETOP HIGH and heat oil. Add beef to pot. Cook uncovered 10 minutes or until browned on all sides. Remove beef from pot.

3. Add remaining oil, carrots, celery, onion, and garlic to pot. Cook uncovered 10 minutes or until vegetables are tender, stirring occasionally. Add tomatoes, wine, broth, thyme, and rosemary and heat to a boil.

4. Return beef to pot. Set to SLOW COOK LOW for 6–8 hours. Cover and cook until beef is fork-tender.

5. Remove beef to cutting board. Stir butter and remaining flour in bowl. Stir butter mixture into pot. Set to STOVETOP HIGH. Cook uncovered 2 minutes or until gravy is thickened. Serve beef with gravy.

**NINJA** TIME-SAVER TIP

Cook pot roast in about half the time: Set pot to SLOW COOK HIGH for 4–5 hours.

 STOVETOP

# LOW COUNTRY SHRIMP BOIL

A delicious Carolina favorite that is perfect for a quick 30-minute weekday meal. Serve with your favorite vegetable or salad.

**PREP:** 10 minutes • **COOK:** 20 minutes • **SERVINGS:** 6–8

## Ingredients

**2 cups clam juice**

**1½ pounds small red potatoes**

**1½ pounds gold potatoes**

**5 or 6 ears corn cut into 1- to 2-inch pieces**

**1½ pounds large shell-on shrimp (16–20 count)**

**6 andouille sausages (12 ounces) cut into ½-inch slices**

**3 bay leaves**

**1 tablespoon Old Bay Seasoning**

**1 tablespoon minced garlic**

## Directions

**1.** Set pot to STOVETOP HIGH. Add all ingredients to pot, except shrimp. Cover and cook 17 minutes.

**2.** Add shrimp, cover, and cook 3 minutes more. Serve immediately.

**NINJA** SERVING TIP

Feel free to substitute 2 cups water, beer, or stock for 2 cups clam juice.

Entrées

# ARROZ CON POLLO

Slow cooker chicken and rice, Spanish-style. Take a little siesta while it is cooking.

**PREP:** 20 minutes • **COOK:** 2½ hours • **SERVINGS:** 4–6

## Ingredients

4 tablespoons canola oil

2 teaspoons salt

1 teaspoon garlic powder

½ teaspoon cumin

¼ teaspoon pepper

¼ teaspoon cayenne pepper

½ teaspoon dry mustard

1 4-pound whole chicken cut into 8 pieces

1 medium onion, diced

2 cloves garlic, minced

1 medium green pepper, diced

1 medium red pepper, diced

1½ cups low-sodium chicken stock

½ cup tomato sauce

salt and pepper to taste

1½ cups long-grain rice

## Directions

1. Set pot to STOVETOP HIGH. Add canola oil. Meanwhile, combine salt, garlic powder, cumin, pepper, cayenne pepper, and mustard to form a rub. Season chicken pieces with rub.

2. Add chicken and sear 3 minutes. Flip and sear 3 more minutes to brown, then remove from pot. Do this in two steps to avoid crowding.

3. Once oil is heated, sear chicken on both sides, approximately 3 minutes per side.

4. Add onion, garlic, and peppers, and sauté 2 minutes, stirring often.

5. Add chicken stock, tomato sauce, salt, and pepper and stir to incorporate.

6. Stir in rice, top with browned chicken, and cover.

7. Set pot to SLOW COOKER HIGH for 2½ hours. Serve immediately.

**NINJA** SERVING TIP

Traditionally this dish contains saffron, which is quite pricey, but if you have it, add a few threads in step 5 and then watch the color change.

149

 STOVETOP

# BRAISED SHORT RIBS WITH PANCETTA

These short ribs are perfect with Parmigiano-Reggiano Polenta
(page 185) and Roasted Brussels Sprouts (page 184).

**PREP:** 15 minutes • **COOK:** 3 hours • **SERVINGS:** 8

## Ingredients

4 pounds boneless short ribs

salt and pepper

about 3 tablespoons vegetable oil

½ pound pancetta, cut into ½-inch
pieces

2 medium red onions, sliced into
½-inch rounds

2 tablespoons tomato paste

2 bottles Guinness

¼ cup sherry wine vinegar

2 cups beef stock
(1 can, and some water is fine)

2 sprigs fresh rosemary, finely
minced

## Directions

**1.** Season short ribs with salt and pepper.

**2.** Set pot to STOVETOP HIGH. Heat the oil until very hot. Sear the
ribs in two batches, until brown on all sides. Remove the ribs
from the pot and pour off the excess oil, but don't clean the pan.

**3.** Add the pancetta and cook until it has rendered its fat, about
5 minutes. Add the onions and cook until lightly browned, about
6 minutes. Add the tomato paste and cook, stirring, for another
2 minutes. Add the beer, vinegar, beef stock, and ribs. Bring the
liquid to a boil. Cover the pot and set to STOVETOP LOW for about
2 hours and 15 minutes (if mixture begins to boil, remove lid).

**4.** Remove ribs from the pot and reserve. Set to STOVETOP HIGH
and bring the liquid to a boil and cook until it's reduced by one-
third. Taste and adjust seasonings and flavors as desired. Add
ribs back to the sauce and set to STOVETOP LOW
to heat ribs through.

**5.** Garnish with rosemary
and serve immediately.

**NINJA** TIME-SAVING TIP

Prepare this dish in the morning and set
to SLOW COOK LOW for 8 hours. Then
just serve at dinnertime. The ribs will be
even more tender cooked low and slow.

 OVEN

# TEX-MEX MEATLOAF

Use your favorite corn tortilla chips in a completely new way; the flavor really permeates throughout the meatloaf.

**PREP:** 10 minutes • **COOK:** 1 hour • **SERVINGS:** 6–8

## Ingredients

3 pounds ground beef

2 teaspoons chopped garlic

1 cup fresh mild salsa, drained, liquid reserved

3 teaspoons salt

1½ teaspoons pepper

2 teaspoons ground mustard

1 cup crushed corn tortilla chips

2 large eggs

## Directions

**1.** Set OVEN to 400°F and set time to 1 hour.

**2.** Combine all ingredients in a large bowl.

**3.** Spray roasting pan with oil.

**4.** Form a dome-shaped meatloaf on roasting pan, leaving a ½-inch border.

**5.** Place pan in pot, cover, and cook 1 hour. Remove and let stand 10 minutes. Slice and serve.

### NINJA SERVING TIP

Leftovers? Crumble leftover meatloaf over tortilla chips placed on the roasting pan. Add salsa and cheese and bake on OVEN at 350°F, until hot, about 10 minutes, for quick nachos.

 OVEN

Entrées

# PANKO PARMESAN-CRUSTED TILAPIA

Fish goes right from the freezer to the pot—no need to waste time thawing! The efficient cooking process gives you a crunchy crust and tender, flaky fish in no time!

**PREP:** 5 minutes • **COOK:** 40 minutes • **SERVINGS:** 4

## Ingredients

½ **cup seasoned panko bread crumbs**

2 **tablespoons grated Parmesan cheese**

¼ **teaspoon paprika**

1 **package (12 ounces) frozen tilapia fillets (4 fillets)**

2 **tablespoons Dijon-style mustard**

## Directions

**1.** Stir bread crumbs, cheese, and paprika on plate.

**2.** Place unwrapped frozen fish into multi-purpose pan, overlapping edges slightly to fit. Brush frozen fish with mustard. Sprinkle with bread crumb mixture. Place pan into top of pot. Set OVEN to 425°F for 40 minutes. Cover and cook until fish flakes easily when tested with fork.

**NINJA** SERVING TIP

Serve this meal with a side of pasta or rice and green bean salad from the deli counter.

**STOVETOP/SLOW COOK**

# THAI BARBECUE PORK BABY BACK RIBS

Ribs are defined by how they are cut: Baby back ribs are close to the loin, St. Louis-style ribs are the cut below the baby back rib, rib tips are below St. Louis, and country style is cut from the shoulder area of the pig.

**PREP:** 4 hours, 16 minutes • **COOK:** 3 hours, 8 minutes • **SERVINGS:** 2–4

## Ingredients

1 can (13.5 ounces) unsweetened coconut milk

½ cup chopped cilantro

½ cup brown sugar

½ cup chopped shallots

¼ cup tamari or soy sauce

4 cloves garlic, minced

3 tablespoons chopped ginger

1 teaspoon coriander

2 tablespoons lime juice

1 large jalapeño seeded, membrane removed, diced

3½- to 4-pound baby back rib, cut into four pieces

salt and pepper to taste

## Directions

1. Combine first 10 ingredients in a food processor and process until smooth, about 1 minute.

2. Place ribs in a ceramic dish. Reserve ½ cup marinade to use as a dipping sauce for the cooked ribs, then cover the ribs with the remaining marinade, cover, and refrigerate at least 4 hours.

3. Set pot to STOVETOP HIGH.

4. Remove the ribs from the marinade and season with salt and pepper.

5. Add ribs to pot and sear 4 minutes. Flip and sear 4 minutes to brown more, then pour marinade over ribs and cover.

6. Set pot to SLOW COOKER HIGH for 3 hours. Serve immediately with reserved dipping sauce.

**NINJA** SERVING TIP

This marinade can be used for other cuts of pork. Just remember, the thicker the cut, the longer the marinade time.

# ITALIAN POT ROAST

Searing the pot roast before using the slow cooker function gives this dish a richer, more complex flavor.

**PREP:** 20 minutes • **COOK:** 2 hours, 50 minutes • **SERVINGS:** 4–6

## Ingredients

2 tablespoons olive oil

4 pounds chuck roast or rump roast

salt and pepper to taste

2 cups chopped carrots

2 cups chopped onion

1 cup chopped green pepper

1 cup chopped red pepper

3 cloves garlic, minced

1 can (28 ounces) whole peeled
  tomatoes, chopped

1½ cups tomato sauce

1 cup medium-bodied Italian red
  wine

1 bay leaf

½ tablespoon oregano

1 tablespoon chopped Italian flat-
  leaf parsley

## Directions

**1.** Set pot to STOVETOP HIGH and add olive oil. Season roast with salt and pepper, then put in pot and sear all sides to brown, about 10 minutes. Meanwhile mix together remaining ingredients.

**2.** Set pot to SLOW COOK HIGH. Add mixture to pot, cover, and cook for 2½ hours.

**3.** Remove roast and let rest 10 minutes. Slice and serve with sauce and vegetables.

**NINJA** SERVING TIP

Cube the roast before browning, add 1 pound Red Bliss potatoes, and turn this dish into an Italian stew.

**Entrées**

# COD WITH ORANGE GLAZE & SNAP PEAS

Cod is a firm, white fish that stands up beautifully to the gingered orange glaze. The sauce reduces to a glaze in the bottom of the pot while sugar snap peas steam on the rack, creating an especially delicious dinner.

**PREP:** 10 minutes • **COOK:** 20 minutes • **SERVINGS:** 4

## Ingredients

2 teaspoons canola oil

1 teaspoon ground ginger

2 cloves garlic, minced

1 bunch green onions, sliced

⅔ cup orange juice

⅓ cup water

2 teaspoons reduced-sodium soy sauce

1 tablespoon sugar

4 frozen uncooked cod fillets, 1-inch thick

2 cups sugar snap peas

## Directions

1. Pour oil into pot. Set to STOVETOP HIGH and heat oil. Add ginger, garlic, and half the green onions to pot. Cook uncovered 3 minutes or until garlic is tender, stirring occasionally.

2. Stir orange juice, water, soy sauce, and sugar into pot. Place frozen fish into the multi-purpose pan. Place rack into pot. Place pan on rack. Set OVEN to 325°F for 15 minutes. Cover and cook 5 minutes.

3. Place snap peas on top of fish. Cover and cook 5 minutes or until fish flakes easily when tested with fork and snap peas are tender-crisp, checking for doneness after 3 minutes of cooking time. Serve fish and snap peas with orange sauce and sprinkle with remaining green onions.

**NINJA** SERVING TIP

Frozen cod comes in different weights and thicknesses. For thicker fish, add an additional ½ cup water or orange juice to the glaze and add 2–4 minutes to the cooking time.

 **STOVETOP**

# ORANGE CHICKEN WITH SOBA NOODLES

**By using orange marmalade in this traditional Hunan recipe, we have eliminated the need to peel and zest oranges.**

**PREP:** 20 minutes • **COOK:** 16–20 minutes • **SERVINGS:** 4

## Ingredients

8 ounces dried soba noodles

1 tablespoon canola oil

1 pound boneless, skinless chicken breast, cut into ½-inch cubes

1 tablespoon cornstarch

1 medium onion, cut in half, then sliced ¼ inch

1 large green pepper, sliced ¼ inch

½ cup orange juice

½ cup orange marmalade

¼ cup light brown sugar

2 tablespoons rice vinegar

1 tablespoon cornstarch

½ teaspoon ground ginger

2 teaspoons sesame oil

½ cup scallions

## Directions

**1.** Set pot to STOVETOP HIGH, add water, and bring to a boil. Add soba noodles and cook 4 minutes, drain, and keep warm.

**2.** Add 2 teaspoons canola oil. Meanwhile, toss cubed chicken breast with 1 tablespoon cornstarch.

**3.** Add cubed chicken and stir-fry 7–8 minutes. Remove and keep warm. Add 1 teaspoon canola oil.

**4.** Add sliced peppers and onions and stir-fry 3–4 minutes. Remove and keep warm. Meanwhile, whisk together orange juice, marmalade, brown sugar, vinegar, cornstarch, and ginger and cook 1–2 minutes.

**5.** Return chicken, vegetables, and noodles to pot. Add sesame oil and scallions, stir well to coat, heat 1–2 minutes, and serve immediately.

 **NINJA** SERVING TIP

To spice up this dish, add 1 teaspoon red pepper flakes to the sauce.

STOVETOP

# CHICKEN WITH MANGO AVOCADO SALSA

When the flavors from the spices blend and hit the hot pot for the first time, the aromas really accentuate the kitchen; you will be inspired to put on salsa music.

**PREP:** 20 minutes  •  **COOK:** 12–16 minutes  •  **SERVINGS:** 4

## Ingredients

2 tablespoons olive oil

1 tablespoon smoked paprika

1 teaspoon ground cumin

1 teaspoon ground coriander

2 teaspoons garlic salt

4 6-ounce chicken breasts

1 ripe avocado, diced

1 medium ripe mango, diced

½ medium red pepper, diced

1 clove garlic, minced

¼ cup diced red onion

2 tablespoons fresh lime juice

1 tablespoon chopped cilantro

## Directions

1. Set pot to STOVETOP HIGH and add 1 tablespoon olive oil. Meanwhile, mix together paprika, cumin, coriander, and garlic salt.

2. Season the chicken breasts with the spice blend.

3. Add chicken breasts to unit, sear, cover, and cook 6–8 minutes. Flip, sear, cover, and cook 6–8 minutes more.

4. For salsa, mix together avocado, mango, red pepper, garlic, onion, lime juice, 1 tablespoon olive oil, and cilantro.

5. Plate chicken breast, topped with salsa.

**NINJA** SERVING TIP

Slice up the chicken and wrap this tasty combination in a soft tortilla. Add chopped lettuce and shredded Mexican cheese, and you have an easy fajita kind of night.

Entrées

# DRY-RUBBED ROASTED TURKEY TENDERLOINS WITH SWEET CHILI

A spiced, sweet dry rub seasons the turkey before it's seared in the pot. It's pan-roasting, but with an all-in-one appliance that doesn't heat up your kitchen!

**PREP:** 10 minutes • **COOK:** 30 minutes • **SERVINGS:** 6

## Ingredients

- **1 tablespoon sugar**
- **1 teaspoon salt**
- **1 teaspoon ground cinnamon**
- **1 teaspoon garlic powder**
- **½ teaspoon dried thyme leaves, crushed**
- **¼ teaspoon ground cumin**
- **1 package (24 ounces) boneless turkey breast tenderloins**
- **2 tablespoons olive oil**
- **⅓ cup sweet chili sauce**
- **1 teaspoon Worcestershire sauce**

## Directions

1. Stir sugar, salt, cinnamon, garlic powder, thyme, and cumin in bowl. Brush turkey with 1 tablespoon oil. Rub turkey with sugar mixture.

2. Pour remaining oil into pot. Set to STOVETOP HIGH and heat oil. Add turkey to pot. Cook uncovered 15 minutes or until browned on both sides. Remove turkey from pot.

3. Place rack into pot. Place turkey on rack. Set OVEN to 350°F for 10 minutes, checking after 8 minutes. Cover and cook until turkey is cooked through. Remove turkey from pot and let stand 5 minutes before slicing.

4. Stir chili sauce and Worcestershire sauce in bowl. Serve chili sauce mixture with turkey.

 **NINJA** SERVING TIP

Substitute chicken or pork tenderloins for turkey if desired.

 **STOVETOP/STEAM OVEN**

# BEEF TENDERLOIN WITH RED WINE REDUCTION

A simple and delicious entrée that will definitely impress your guests. We recommend searing after steam roasting to ensure optimal browning.

**PREP:** 10 minutes • **COOK:** 1 hour, 10 minutes • **SERVINGS:** 10

## Ingredients

1 6-pound whole beef tenderloin, trimmed

5 cloves garlic, peeled and cut into thin pieces

kosher salt and pepper

3 cups beef broth

2 bay leaves

3 tablespoons butter

1 tablespoon olive oil

1 bottle red wine, merlot or pinot noir preferred (light-bodied)

## Directions

1. Pat dry whole beef tenderloin with paper towels. Fold the small end of the beef tenderloin under and tie with cooking twine. Cut the meat through in half to make two equal-sized roasts to fit in pot.

2. With a small, thin knife, make small slits in meat and stud with garlic on all sides. Season with salt and pepper.

3. Add broth and bay leaves to pot, place meat on rack, place in pot, and cover. Set OVEN to 350°F for 30 minutes. Cook until meat reaches 120°F internal temperature. Remove meat from rack. Pour off steam-roasting liquid. Add 1 tablespoon butter and oil to pot. Set to STOVETOP HIGH and sear meat on all sides until meat is 130°F, approximately 15 minutes.

4. Remove meat and place on platter to rest until temperature reaches internal temperature of 140°F.

5. To make red wine reduction, pour red wine into pot and set to STOVETOP HIGH. Reduce to half the liquid. Season with salt and pepper. Whisk in 2 tablespoons butter and pour into a gravy boat. To serve, cut meat into 1-inch medallions and serve with red wine reduction.

# PORK WITH CURRY COCONUT

This recipe has a delicious combination of curry powder and coconut milk for sweet and savory flavors.

**PREP:** 15 minutes • **COOK:** 2 hours, 6 minutes • **SERVINGS:** 4–6

## Ingredients

3 tablespoons olive oil

2 tablespoons minced ginger

½ teaspoon coriander

½ teaspoon cardamom

2 tablespoons curry powder, yellow preferably

4 pounds pork loin

1 cup chopped onion

4 cloves garlic, minced

2 cans (13.5 ounces) coconut milk

salt and pepper to taste

## Directions

1. Set pot to STOVETOP HIGH, and add olive oil. Meanwhile, combine ginger, coriander, cardamom, and curry powder and rub over pork loin.

2. Add pork loin and sear 2–3 minutes. Flip, sear 2–3 minutes to brown, and remove from pot.

3. Add onion and garlic and sauté 2 minutes, stirring often. Add coconut milk to pot. Place rack in pot and seared pork loin on rack.

4. Turn pot to SLOW COOKER HIGH for 2 hours, cover, and cook.

5. Turn pot off. Remove pork loin, let rest 10 minutes, slice, and serve with sauce.

**NINJA** SERVING TIP

Curry paste is more complex than curry powder and generally spicy, so if you want to kick this dish up a notch, whisk ¼ cup curry paste into the coconut milk and skip the curry powder.

 OVEN

# CAJUN SPICE-RUBBED COUNTRY-STYLE PORK RIBS

Three ingredients are all you need to make these mouth-watering ribs. The pot surrounds the meat with even heat, yielding fork-tender pork every time.

**PREP:** 5 minutes • **COOK:** 2 hours • **SERVINGS:** 6

## Ingredients

3 tablespoons Cajun seasoning

2 tablespoons packed light brown sugar

3 pounds bone-in country-style pork ribs

2 cups water

## Directions

1. Stir Cajun seasoning and brown sugar in bowl. Rub pork with seasoning mixture.

2. Pour water into pot. Place rack into pot. Place pork on rack. Place rack into pot. Set OVEN to 375°F for 2 hours. Cover and cook until pork is fork-tender.

**NINJA** SERVING TIP

Serve with macaroni and cheese, sliced tomatoes, and watermelon slices for dessert.

 **STOVETOP**

# PINEAPPLE CASHEW SHRIMP

This fresh Asian dish combines great flavors of sesame, ginger, and tropical pineapple. Serve with your favorite rice, and done in 20 minutes!

**PREP:** 12 minutes • **COOK:** 5–7 minutes • **SERVINGS:** 4

## Ingredients

2 tablespoons canola oil

1 can (20 ounces) pineapple chunks, drained, liquid reserved

3 teaspoons cornstarch

3 tablespoons soy sauce or tamari sauce

2 teaspoons ginger root, grated or microplaned

1 pound large shrimp (16–20, peeled and deveined)

1 cup cashews, unsalted or lightly salted

1 can (8 ounces) sliced water chestnuts, drained

2 green onions sliced, both green and white parts

## Directions

1. Set pot to STOVETOP HIGH and add canola oil. Meanwhile, blend pineapple juice, cornstarch, and soy sauce or tamari sauce and set aside.

2. Add shrimp and ginger, and sauté 1 minute, stirring.

3. Add cashews and water chestnuts and stir. Cover and cook 2–3 minutes.

4. Add pineapple and sauce and stir. Cover and cook 2–3 minutes. Serve immediately, garnished with green onions.

**NINJA** SERVING TIP

If you have an overripe golden pineapple, substitute it for the canned stuff. Add its juices to a 6-ounce can of pineapple juice for the sauce.

 OVEN

# OLIVE TAPENADE-CRUSTED SWORDFISH

This tapenade is simple, but the flavors really add that zip to elevate this fish and make it the star of any dinner.

**PREP:** 10 minutes • **COOK:** 22 minutes • **SERVINGS:** 4

## Ingredients

2 cloves garlic, minced

½ medium onion, chunked

1 cup pitted kalamata olives, drained

4 halves sun-dried tomatoes

⅛ cup parsley

2 tablespoons olive oil

4 4-ounce swordfish fillets

salt and pepper to taste

## Directions

**1.** Add garlic and onions to food processor and pulse to mince. Add olives, sun-dried tomatoes, parsley, and olive oil and pulse to desired texture.

**2.** Season swordfish with salt and pepper and coat with tapenade.

**3.** Add encrusted swordfish to pot, set OVEN to 350°F, and bake 22 minutes. Serve immediately.

**NINJA** SERVING TIP

Serve this Mediterranean-inspired fish on a bed of baby spinach for a warm salad combination that is as good for you as it is beautiful.

CRUSTY, CHEESY POTATOES AU GRATIN

# CHAPTER 7:
# Side Dishes

STEAM OVEN/SLOW COOK

# GARLICKY MASHED POTATOES

These creamy garlic mashed potatoes not only taste better than your old standby, but they are easier to make, too! The potatoes and garlic cook in the perfect amount of water, so there is no need to drain them before mashing.

**PREP:** 10 minutes • **COOK:** 30 minutes • **SERVINGS:** 12

## Ingredients

**5 pounds russet potatoes, peeled and diced**

**4 cloves garlic, peeled**

**2 cups water**

**½ cup butter, cut up**

**1½ cups hot milk or heavy cream**

**salt and ground black pepper**

## Directions

1. Place potatoes, garlic, and water into pot. Set OVEN to 350°F for 30 minutes. Cover and cook until potatoes are tender. Turn off pot.

2. Mash potatoes with butter and milk. Season with salt and black pepper. Serve immediately or set to SLOW COOK WARM for 1 hour or until ready to serve.

**NINJA** HEALTHY TIP

Substitute chicken broth for milk or cream and reduce amount of butter to save some calories in a lighter version of this recipe. Yukon Gold potatoes can also be substituted for the russets.

STOVETOP

# Side Dishes

# CURRY TOFU WITH CHICKPEAS & VEGETABLES

Curry powder is a traditional Indian spice mix that typically includes cumin, coriander, pepper, ginger, cardamom, clove, cinnamon, and bay leaf.

**PREP:** 15 minutes • **COOK:** 10 minutes • **SERVINGS:** 6–8

## Ingredients

3 tablespoons canola oil

1 package extra-firm tofu, drained and dried, cut into 1-inch pieces

3 tablespoons curry powder

½ head broccoli, cut into florets

1 medium green pepper, sliced 1-inch thick

1 can (15 ounces) chickpeas, drained and rinsed

1 small onion, sliced 1-inch thick

1 can (20 ounces) diced tomatoes

2 cups chopped kale

8 ounces snap peas

## Directions

1. Set pot to STOVETOP HIGH. Meanwhile, in a large mixing bowl, combine oil, tofu, and 2 tablespoons curry powder and toss to coat.

2. Add tofu and sauté 4 minutes.

3. Add broccoli, green pepper, chickpeas, onion, tomatoes, kale, and the remaining ⅓ tablespoon curry powder to the pot, lightly toss with tofu, cover, and cook 5 minutes.

4. Add snap peas to pot, cover, and cook 2 minutes. Serve immediately.

**NINJA** SERVING TIP

For a spicier dish, add some heat with a hot pepper instead of a bell pepper.

172

 **OVEN**

# EGGPLANT & ARTICHOKE PARMESAN

Enjoy flavors of eggplant Parmesan without all the work —
just assemble and bake! Eggplant and artichokes in a chunky
tomato sauce are topped with bread crumbs and melted
cheese — delicious!

**PREP:** 10 minutes • **COOK:** 50 minutes • **SERVINGS:** 6

## Ingredients

- 1 large eggplant (about 1½ pounds), cut in ¾-inch pieces
- 1 jar (about 24 ounces) marinara sauce
- 1 can (14.5 ounces) diced tomatoes, undrained
- 1 can (about 14 ounces) artichoke hearts, rinsed, drained, and quartered
- 1 small onion, chopped
- ½ cup Italian-seasoned dry bread crumbs
- 1 cup shredded mozzarella cheese
- ½ cup grated Parmesan cheese

## Directions

1. Place eggplant, sauce, tomatoes, artichokes, and onion in pot. Set OVEN to 325°F for 50 minutes. Cover and cook 40 minutes, stirring once halfway through cooking time.

2. Top with bread crumbs and cheeses. Cover and cook 10 minutes or until cheese is melted.

**NINJA** SERVING TIP

This tastes wonderful topped with ¼ cup toasted pine nuts.

 **STOVETOP/OVEN**

# SEA SALT & CHILI ROASTED SWEET POTATO STRIPS

These crisp-on-the-outside, tender-on-the-inside sweet potato strips are sure to go fast at the table! The trick is to sear one side, then flip and bake. The seasonings add a spicy kick!

**PREP:** 10 minutes • **COOK:** 25 minutes • **SERVINGS:** 4

## Ingredients

2 sweet potatoes (about 1¼ pounds), peeled and cut lengthwise into ½-inch slices, then into ½-inch strips

3 tablespoons olive oil

1½ teaspoons sea salt

½ teaspoon chili powder

## Directions

1. Stir potatoes, olive oil, salt, and chili powder in a bowl.

2. Place potato mixture into pot, arranging potatoes in single layer. Set to STOVETOP HIGH. Cook uncovered 10 minutes or until potatoes are lightly browned on bottom. Turn potatoes over. Set OVEN to 325°F for 15 minutes. Cover and cook until potatoes are browned and tender.

**NINJA** SERVING TIP

Serve with ketchup or sour cream for dipping.

STOVETOP/OVEN

# SCALLOPED POTATOES WITH MAPLE CREAM

The savory sweet cream sauce makes this a decadent dish. Potatoes and sweet potatoes provide a twist on traditional scalloped potatoes.

**PREP:** 10 minutes • **COOK:** 55 minutes • **SERVINGS:** 8

## Ingredients

cooking spray

4 large sweet potatoes (about 2 pounds), peeled and thinly sliced

4 large russet potatoes (about 2 pounds), peeled and thinly sliced

1½ cups heavy cream

½ cup pure maple syrup

1 tablespoon minced fresh rosemary leaves

1 teaspoon salt

¼ teaspoon ground black pepper

## Directions

**1.** Spray the multi-purpose pan with cooking spray. Place half the sweet potatoes into pot. Top with half the russet potatoes. Repeat layers.

**2.** Stir cream, syrup, rosemary, salt, and black pepper in a bowl. Pour cream mixture over potatoes. Set OVEN to 275°F for 50 minutes. Cover and cook until potatoes are tender. Set to STOVETOP HIGH. Cook 5 minutes or until potatoes are golden brown on bottom.

**3.** Invert potatoes onto serving platter.

## NINJA SERVING TIP

Serve a twist on this recipe at your Thanksgiving table! Substitute additional sweet potatoes for the russet potatoes. Top cooked sweet potato mixture with ½ cup toasted pecan pieces before serving.

 STOVETOP

# BUTTERNUT SQUASH RISOTTO WITH BACON & SAGE

The butternut squash gives this risotto a lovely golden color. It cooks to creamy perfection in the pot with bacon and fresh sage.

**PREP:** 25 minutes • **COOK:** 1 hour, 5 minutes • **SERVINGS:** 6

## Ingredients

1 tablespoon olive oil

2 medium onions, chopped

4 strips bacon, chopped

2 tablespoons chopped fresh sage leaves

1 cup uncooked Arborio rice

½ teaspoon salt

¼ teaspoon ground black pepper

4 cups chicken broth

2 cups peeled and chopped fresh butternut squash

¼ cup grated Parmesan cheese

## Directions

1. Pour oil into pot. Set to STOVETOP HIGH and heat oil. Add onions, bacon, and sage to pot. Cook uncovered 10 minutes or until onions are tender, stirring occasionally. Stir rice, salt, and black pepper into pot. Cook uncovered 5 minutes, stirring often. Stir in broth. Cook 10 minutes.

2. Stir squash into pot. Set to STOVETOP LOW. Cover and cook 20 minutes or until rice and squash are tender.

3. Stir cheese into pot. Set to STOVETOP HIGH. Cook uncovered 10 minutes or until liquid is absorbed but mixture is creamy, stirring occasionally.

**NINJA** SERVING TIP

Serve sprinkled with additional chopped fresh sage leaves, if desired.

 **STOVETOP**

# GREEN BEAN RAGOUT

While ragouts are typically slow cooked over low heat, we have adapted this recipe for your hectic modern lifestyle.

**PREP:** 15 minutes • **COOK:** 10–15 minutes • **SERVINGS:** 4–6

## Ingredients

2 tablespoons olive oil

1 medium onion, chopped

1 fennel bulb, cored and sliced
½-inch thick

·1 tablespoon garlic, minced

4 ounces wild mushroom medley

1 can (14.5 ounces) fire-roasted
tomatoes

1 pound green beans, cut 1-inch
length

1 teaspoon dry thyme

1 tablespoon lime juice

salt and pepper to taste

## Directions

**1.** Set pot to STOVETOP HIGH and add oil. Add onion and fennel, cover, and cook 3 minutes, stirring occasionally.

**2.** Add garlic and mushrooms and stir. Cover and cook 2 minutes, stirring occasionally.

**3.** Add fire-roasted diced tomatoes, green beans, thyme, and lime juice, stirring. Cover and cook 2 minutes.

**4.** Season with salt and pepper and serve immediately.

**NINJA** SERVING TIP

If it is tomato season in your area, dice up 2 cups of tomatoes and skip the canned stuff.

**STOVETOP/SLOW COOK**

# RATATOUILLE

Sautéing the vegetables in the pot first adds an extra layer of flavor to this French stewed vegetable dish. Eggplant, zucchini, peppers, and tomatoes simmer until meltingly tender with garlic, basil, and oregano.

**PREP:** 20 minutes • **COOK:** 4 hours, 15 minutes • **SERVINGS:** 10

## Ingredients

2 tablespoons olive oil

1 medium onion, chopped

3 cloves garlic, sliced

1 eggplant (about 1½ pounds), cut into 1-inch pieces

2 medium zucchini, cut into 1-inch pieces

2 red peppers, cut into 1-inch pieces

1 teaspoon salt

1 can (28 ounces) diced tomatoes, undrained

1 tablespoon tomato paste

½ teaspoon each ground black pepper and dried oregano leaves, crushed

¼ cup chopped fresh basil leaves

## Directions

1. Pour oil into pot. Set to STOVETOP HIGH and heat oil. Add onion to pot. Cook uncovered 5 minutes or until onion is tender, stirring occasionally. Add garlic, eggplant, zucchini, peppers, and salt to pot. Cook 5 minutes or until vegetables are tender-crisp.

2. Stir tomatoes, tomato paste, black pepper, and oregano into pot. Set to SLOW COOK HIGH for 4–5 hours. Cover and cook until vegetables are tender. Stir in basil.

**NINJA** SERVING TIP

Serve ratatouille as a side dish or toss with pasta and cheese for a main dish.

 STOVETOP

# GNOCCHI WITH ASPARAGUS

The great asparagus debate: thin or thick? Thin takes less time to cook, so thin wins with me. Look for tight heads and juicy bottoms; this indicates freshness.

**PREP:** 10 minutes  •  **COOK:** 16–17 minutes  •  **SERVINGS:** 6–8

## Ingredients

**4½ cups water**

**1 bunch asparagus, trimmed and cut into ½-inch pieces**

**16 ounces gnocchi**

**1 tablespoon olive oil**

**1 garlic clove, sliced**

**¼ cup pine nuts**

**½ cup Asiago cheese, shredded**

## Directions

**1.** Set pot to STOVETOP HIGH. Add ½ cup water and bring to a boil. Add asparagus, blanch for 2 minutes, drain, and reserve cooking water.

**2.** Add 4 cups water and gnocchi, bring to a boil, and cook 8 minutes. Drain and keep warm.

**3.** Set pot to STOVETOP LOW and add olive oil.

**4.** Add garlic and pine nuts and sauté 3–4 minutes until light brown. Add asparagus, reserved cooking liquid, gnocchi, and Asiago cheese. Sauté 3 minutes to heat through, season with salt and pepper, and serve immediately.

### NINJA SERVING TIP

Add smoked salmon after garlic and pine nuts, cover, and let sit for 2 minutes to heat salmon; serve as a nice brunch accompaniment.

 **S T O V E T O P / O V E N**

# CAULIFLOWER MAC & CHEESE

Have your mac and cheese and eat it too with this fiber-rich low-carb comfort food.

**PREP:** 10 minutes • **COOK:** 10 minutes • **SERVINGS:** 4–6

## Ingredients

1 head cauliflower, cut into florets

1 jar (12 ounces) Alfredo sauce

1 cup shredded Gruyére cheese

1½ cups shredded Parmesan cheese

1 teaspoon cumin

½ teaspoon salt

⅛ teaspoon pepper

¼ cup panko bread crumbs (optional)

## Directions

**1.** Set pot to STOVETOP HIGH.

**2.** Add cauliflower, Alfredo sauce, ½ cup Gruyére cheese, 1 cup Parmesan cheese, cumin, salt, and pepper, stir, and cook 5 minutes.

**3.** Top cauliflower with remaining cheese and bread crumbs, cover, and cook 5 minutes. Serve immediately.

**NINJA** SERVING TIP

Substitute the cauliflower with the broccoli cauliflower hybrid called romaneso for a colorful, beautiful dish.

 **STOVETOP**

# PORK & BEANS

Sure, it's easier to just open a can of pork and beans, but this recipe is pretty easy too and might just make you retire that can opener.

**PREP:** 10 minutes  •  **COOK:** 20 minutes  •  **SERVINGS:** 4

## Ingredients

1 tablespoon olive oil

½ pound pork loin, cubed

1 small onion, diced

2 cups tomato sauce

½ cup brown sugar

2 tablespoons Worcestershire sauce

3 tablespoons red wine vinegar

3 tablespoons Dijon mustard

2 cans (28 ounces each) butter beans, strained

## Directions

**1.** Set pot to STOVETOP HIGH and add olive oil.

**2.** Add pork and onion, sauté, cover, and cook 10 minutes, stirring occasionally.

**3.** Add tomato sauce, brown sugar, Worcestershire sauce, red wine vinegar, mustard, and butter beans and stir. Cover, and cook 20 minutes, stirring occasionally. Serve immediately.

**NINJA** SERVING TIP

For added spice, use andouille sausage instead of the pork loin.

 **OVEN**

# CRUSTY, CHEESY POTATOES AU GRATIN

Cream and Gruyère cheese are the stars in this decadent dish. Potatoes absorb the flavors as they cook to tenderness.

**PREP:** 15 minutes • **COOK:** 1 hour • **SERVINGS:** 4

## Ingredients

**1 cup shredded Gruyère or Cheddar cheese (about 4 ounces)**

**2 large russet potatoes or 4 Yukon Gold potatoes, peeled and thinly sliced**

**2 tablespoons butter, cut into small pieces**

**salt and ground black pepper**

**¾ cup heavy cream**

## Directions

**1.** Spray multi-purpose pan with vegetable spray.

**2.** Layer cheese, potatoes, and butter in the pan as follows: one-fourth cheese, one-third potatoes, half butter. Repeat layers, seasoning with salt and black pepper. Top with remaining ¼ cup cheese. Top with remaining potatoes. Pour cream over potatoes and sprinkle with remaining cheese. Cover pan with foil.

**3.** Place rack into pot. Place pan on rack. Set OVEN to 375°F for 1 hour. Cover and cook until potatoes are tender.

 SERVING TIP

Serve with grilled steaks and spinach and mushroom salad.

 **STOVETOP**

# ROASTED BRUSSELS SPROUTS

When placed in pan cut side down, brussels sprouts will caramelize as they brown and become sweet and tender.

**PREP:** 10 minutes • **COOK:** 20–25 minutes • **SERVINGS:** 4

## Ingredients

**2 tablespoons butter**

**¾ pound brussels sprouts, trimmed and halved lengthwise**

**kosher salt and pepper**

## Directions

**1.** Set pot to STOVETOP HIGH and add butter. When butter has melted, add brussels sprouts, cut side down. Cook 15 minutes or until bottom is browned.

**2.** Set pot to STOVETOP LOW and turn over brussels sprouts. Continue to cook until tender, another 5–10 minutes.

**3.** Season with salt and pepper.

**NINJA** SERVING TIP

For a really great flavor, continue to roast sprouts until dark brown, almost black. The outside will caramelize and become almost sweet.

 **STOVETOP**

# PARMIGIANO-REGGIANO POLENTA

This classic polenta is a great side dish for any kind of comforting stew.

**PREP:** 20 minutes • **COOK:** 30 minutes • **SERVINGS:** 4

## Ingredients

**6 cups water**

**1½ teaspoons kosher salt**

**1½ cups medium-grind stone-ground cornmeal**

**3 tablespoons unsalted butter, cut into large chunks, plus more for final serving**

**¾ cup grated Parmigiano-Reggiano cheese, plus more for final serving**

**freshly ground black pepper**

## Directions

1. Set pot to STOVETOP HIGH. Add water, cover, and bring to a boil. Reduce pot to STOVETOP LOW and add salt. Sprinkling in cornmeal with one hand and using a nonstick-safe whisk in the other, slowly sprinkle in cornmeal grains, whisking constantly to prevent lumps.

2. Cover and cook for 5-minute intervals, then give a vigorous stir with a wooden spoon, scraping out corners well. Continue to cook, stirring every 5 minutes, until cornmeal is soft and smooth, about 30 minutes.

3. Stir in butter and cheese and season with salt and pepper to taste. To serve, add additional butter and cheese if desired.

 **NINJA** SERVING TIP

Sprinkle with additional Parmesan cheese and parsley.

**CARAMEL BAKED APPLES**

# CHAPTER 8:
# Desserts

# BANANA LIME COCONUT BREAD

This tropical quick bread is finished with a decadent topping of butter, brown sugar, fresh lime, coconut, and pecans. Steam baking keeps the bread moist and tender, and the pecans in the topping add a nice crunch!

**PREP:** 10 minutes • **COOK:** 40 minutes • **SERVINGS:** 10

## Ingredients

**cooking spray**

**1 cup all-purpose flour**

**1½ teaspoons baking soda**

**pinch salt**

**4 tablespoons butter**

**½ cup sugar**

**1 egg**

**½ ripe banana, mashed**

**⅔ cup skim milk**

**grated zest and juice of 2 limes**

**1 teaspoon vanilla extract**

**4 cups water**

**⅓ cup chopped toasted pecans**

**⅓ cup sweetened flaked coconut**

**¼ cup packed brown sugar**

## Directions

1. Spray multi-purpose pan with cooking spray. Stir flour, baking soda, and salt in a bowl.

2. Beat 2 tablespoons butter and sugar in another bowl with electric mixer until mixture is creamy. Beat in egg.

3. Stir banana, milk, half the lime zest, half the lime juice, and vanilla extract in another bowl. Stir half the flour mixture and half the banana mixture into butter mixture. Repeat with remaining flour mixture and butter mixture. Pour batter into pan.

4. Pour water into pot. Place rack into pot. Place pan on rack. Set OVEN to 375°F for 40 minutes. Cover and cook until wooden pick inserted in center comes out clean. Remove pan from pot. Let bread cool in pan on cooling rack 10 minutes.

5. Remove rack from pot and pour out water. Stir remaining butter, pecans, coconut, brown sugar, lime zest, and lime juice in pot. Set to STOVETOP HIGH. Cook uncovered 1 minute or until sugar is dissolved. Spoon coconut mixture over bread.

**NINJA** SERVING TIP

This banana bread is great as either a breakfast or a dessert.

# MAPLE PUMPKIN FLAN

These individual custards are perfect served as a special dessert for any autumn get-together. The water in the pot gently cooks the custard, ensuring a creamy texture every time.

**PREP:** 10 minutes • **COOK:** 45 minutes **CHILL:** 4 hours • **SERVINGS:** 4

## Ingredients

½ **cup pure maple syrup**

3 **eggs**

¾ **cup canned pumpkin**

½ **cup milk**

¼ **cup sugar**

1 **teaspoon pumpkin pie spice**

1 **teaspoon vanilla extract**

8 **cups boiling water**

## Directions

**1.** Place 2 tablespoons syrup in each of the four (6-ounce) custard cups.

**2.** Beat eggs, pumpkin, milk, sugar, spice, and vanilla extract. Carefully pour pumpkin mixture into custard cups.

**3.** Pour water into pot. Place rack into pot. Place custard cups on rack (water should cover about ¼ of the bottoms of the custard cups). Set OVEN to 350°F for 45 minutes. Cover and cook until custards are just set. Remove custard cups from pot. Let flans cool in cups on cooling rack 5 minutes.

**4.** Cover custard cups and refrigerate at least 4 hours or overnight. To serve, loosen edges of flans with a knife. Invert onto dessert plates.

 SERVING TIP

Add some orange or lemon zest for a flavorful garnish.

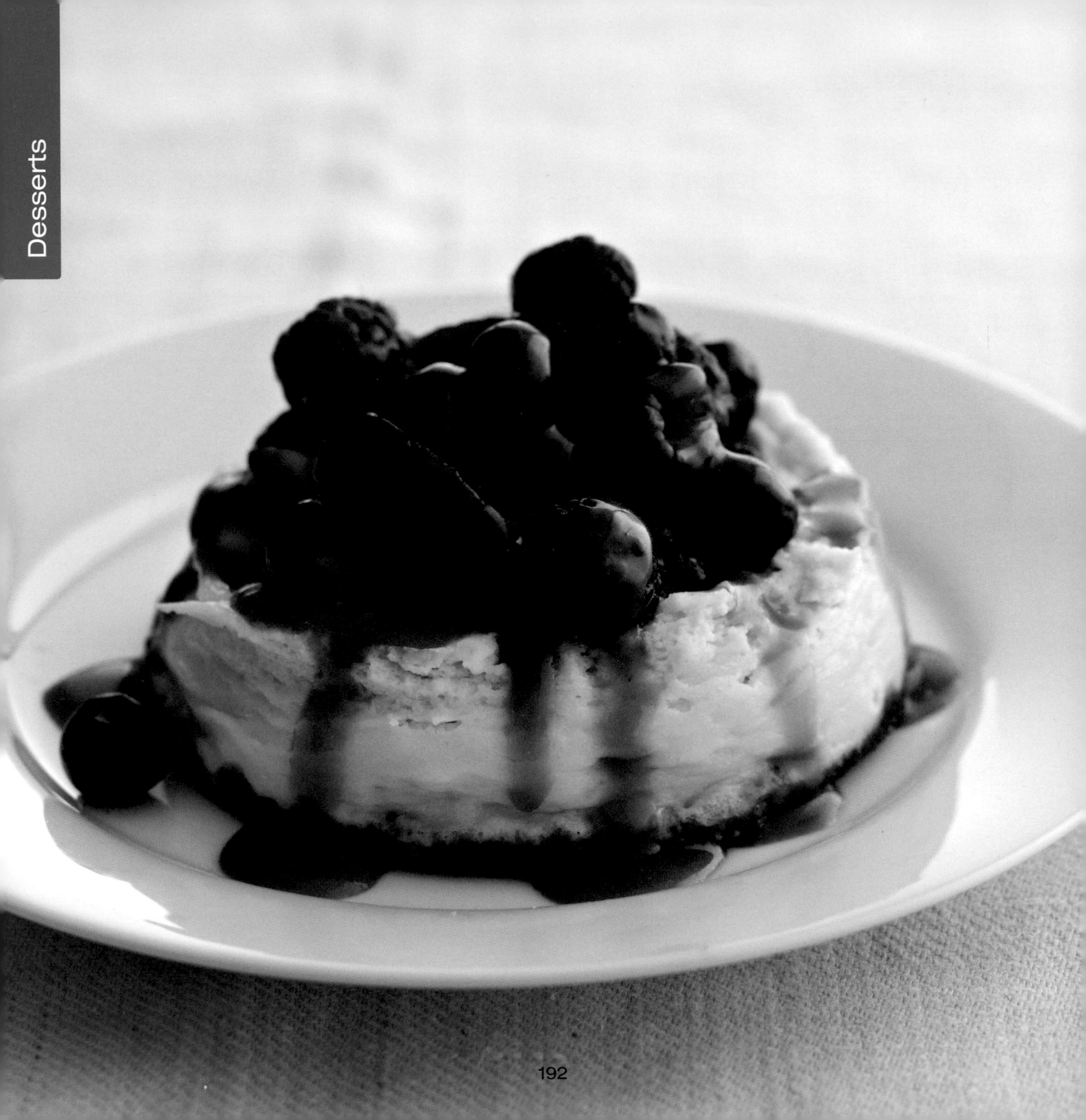

 **STEAM OVEN**

# MINI CHEESECAKES

This creamy cheesecake recipe is simple to put together, and the steam-baking technique ensures great results every time. Unlike traditional cheesecake recipes, the water bath stays in the bottom of the pot, so you don't have to deal with a pan full of hot water.

**PREP:** 15 minutes • **COOK:** 35 minutes **CHILL:** 4 hours • **SERVINGS:** 4

## Ingredients

½ **cup graham cracker crumbs**

**2 tablespoons melted butter**

⅓ **cup sugar**

1½ **8-ounce packages cream cheese, softened**

**1 egg**

**1 teaspoon vanilla extract**

**4 cups water**

## Directions

**1.** Cover outside of two (4-inch) springform pans with foil.

**2.** Stir graham cracker crumbs, butter, and 1 tablespoon sugar in bowl. Press mixture into bottoms of pans.

**3.** Beat cream cheese with remaining sugar in bowl with electric mixer until smooth. Beat in egg and vanilla extract. Pour batter into pans.

**4.** Pour water into pot. Place rack into pot and place filled pans on rack and cover. Set OVEN to 325°F for 35 minutes. Do not lift lid during cooking.

**5.** Remove pans from pot, and let cool. Cover and refrigerate at least 4 hours or overnight.

**NINJA** SERVING TIP

Serve topped with fresh fruit (sliced strawberries, blueberries, or raspberries), fruit preserves, lemon curd, caramel sauce, toasted chopped pecans, or mini chocolate chips.

 **STOVETOP/STEAM OVEN**

# CARAMEL BAKED APPLES

Making caramel sauce sounds difficult — but not with this recipe. You can make the stuffed baked apples and the simple caramel sauce in the same pot — no extra saucepan to clean!

**PREP:** 15 minutes • **COOK:** 35 minutes • **SERVINGS:** 6

## Ingredients

**6 medium apples (about 3 pounds), cored**

**12 vanilla wafer cookies, finely crushed**

**¼ cup butter, melted**

**3 tablespoons raisins**

**½ teaspoon ground cinnamon**

**2 cups water**

**¼ cup packed dark brown sugar**

**18 caramels, unwrapped**

## Directions

**1.** Remove 1 strip of apple peel about 1 inch from top of each apple. Stir cookie crumbs, 2 tablespoons melted butter, raisins, and cinnamon in bowl. Stuff about 1 tablespoon cookie crumb mixture into each apple.

**2.** Stir water, brown sugar, and remaining melted butter in pot. Place rack into pot. Place stuffed apples on rack. Set OVEN to 350°F for 30 minutes. Cover and cook until apples are tender, checking for doneness after 10 minutes of cooking time.

**3.** Carefully remove apples and rack from pot. Add caramels to liquid in pot. Set to STOVETOP LOW. Cook uncovered 5 minutes or until caramels are melted and mixture is smooth, stirring constantly with wooden spoon. Drizzle 2 tablespoons caramel sauce over each apple.

**NINJA** SERVING TIP

Serve the apples and caramel sauce warm with vanilla ice cream or sweetened whipped cream.

 **STEAM OVEN**

# CHOCOLATE PEANUT BUTTER CUPCAKES

**Two favorite flavors are reminiscent of childhood parties and the warmth of home-baked goodies! The pot's consistent heat distribution from the steam keeps the cupcakes cooking evenly.**

**PREP:** 10 minutes • **COOK:** 20 minutes • **SERVINGS:** 6

## Ingredients

½ **cup all-purpose flour**

½ **cup sugar**

2 **tablespoons unsweetened cocoa powder**

¼ **teaspoon baking soda**

¼ **teaspoon salt**

¼ **cup milk**

3 **tablespoons creamy peanut butter**

1 **egg, beaten**

1 **teaspoon vanilla extract**

2 **cups water**

1 **cup prepared chocolate fudge frosting**

## Directions

**1.** Stir flour, sugar, cocoa powder, baking soda, and salt in a bowl. Stir milk, 2 tablespoons peanut butter, egg, and vanilla extract in another bowl. Stir milk mixture into flour mixture.

**2.** Line 6-cup muffin pan with paper liners. Spoon batter into liners.

**3.** Pour water into pot. Place rack in pot and place pan onto rack. Set OVEN to 350°F for 20 minutes. Cover and cook until tops spring back when lightly touched. Remove pan from pot and let cool on cooling rack 15 minutes.

**4.** Stir frosting with remaining peanut butter in bowl. Frost cupcakes.

**NINJA** SERVING TIP

Use peanut butter thinned with a little milk and sugar to frost cupcakes, then drizzle with melted chocolate.

**Desserts**

# APPLE CHERRY PASTRIES WITH PISTACHIOS

A warm compote of apples and dried cherries slow cooks with lemon and sugar before being spooned into pastry cups. A dollop of creamy vanilla pudding and sprinkle of chopped pistachios are the perfect finish!

**PREP:** 35 minutes • **COOK:** 2 hours • **SERVINGS:** 12

## Ingredients

1 lemon

8 apples (about 3 pounds), peeled and cut into ¼-inch slices

½ cup dried cherries

1 cup sugar

1 package (3.4 ounces) vanilla instant pudding and pie filling mix

3 cups cold milk

2 packages (10 ounces each) frozen puff pastry shells, prepared according to package directions, cooled

½ cup shelled pistachio nuts, chopped

## Directions

**1.** Grate ½ teaspoon zest from lemon.

**2.** Stir apples, cherries, sugar, and lemon zest in pot. Set to SLOW COOK HIGH for 2–3 hours. Cover and cook until apples are tender.

**3.** Beat pudding mix and milk in bowl 2 minutes or until mixture is thickened. Divide apple mixture among pastry shells. Top with pudding mixture and sprinkle with nuts.

**NINJA** SERVING TIP

Add different ingredients for a unique dessert: pear, dried cranberries, almonds... the possibilities are endless.

# PASSION FRUIT CRÈME BRÛLÉE

Passionate about crème brûlée? So are we! Try this one and discover a new passion.

**PREP:** 2 hours, 10 minutes • **COOK:** 1 hour • **SERVINGS:** 4

## Ingredients

**6 large passion fruits, cut in half**

**8 egg yolks**

**1½ cups heavy cream**

**2 ounces milk**

**10 tablespoons sugar**

**4 cups water**

## Directions

1. Set OVEN to 350°F and add water. Meanwhile, scoop out the passion fruit into a large mixing bowl. Add egg yolks and 6 tablespoons sugar. Whip the mixture on high 5 minutes, until mixture is frothy and pale in color.

2. Put heavy cream and milk in a microwave-safe bowl and microwave on high 3 minutes. Slowly whisk hot liquid into egg mixture, then pour mixture through a strainer to remove the passion fruit seeds.

3. Place ramekins on rack and fill with mixture. Place the rack in pot and set timer for 1 hour. Cover and bake. Ramekins are ready to remove when custard is set and gently wobbles when moved. Turn pot off.

4. Remove ramekins and allow to cool to room temperature. Cover with plastic wrap and refrigerate 2 hours.

5. When ready to serve, sprinkle remaining sugar equally over top of each ramekin. Using a blowtorch, melt and caramelize the sugar. Cool before serving.

**NINJA** SERVING TIP

Place the ramekins under the broiler for a few minutes if you don't own a blowtorch. Keep an eye on it though; you do not want to burn the sugar.

 **SLOW COOK**

# MEXICAN CHOCOLATE BREAD PUDDING

Cinnamon and chile powder both have antioxidant power and pair perfectly with chocolate.

**PREP:** 2 hours, 15 minutes • **COOK:** 2½ hours • **SERVINGS:** 6–8

## Ingredients

**6 cups day-old challah bread, cubed**

**½ cup granulated sugar**

**⅓ cup cocoa powder**

**1½ teaspoons ground cinnamon**

**1 teaspoon red chile powder**

**¼ salt**

**6 eggs**

**3 cups milk**

**¼ cup heavy cream**

**2 teaspoon vanilla extract**

**1 teaspoon almond extract**

**1 cup chocolate chips**

**whipped cream**

## Directions

**1.** Place the bread into a buttered pot.

**2.** In a small bowl stir together sugar, cocoa powder, cinnamon, red chile powder, and salt until well combined.

**3.** Place eggs, milk, cream, and vanilla and almond extracts into a blender and process on low speed. Add sugar mixture and blend to combine. Pour liquid over bread. Cover and refrigerate 2 hours or overnight.

**4.** Remove cover and stir in chocolate chips. Bring to room temperature, set to SLOW COOK HIGH for 2½ hours, and cook until a knife inserted in the center comes out clean and top is golden brown.

**5.** Invert onto a sheet pan before cutting and serving in bite-sized portions. Top with whipped cream.

 **NINJA** SERVING TIP

Make ahead and refrigerate.
This makes a great cold dish.

**STEAM OVEN**

# LIGHT KIWI LIME ANGEL FOOD CUPCAKES

These fun desserts are only 15 calories each! Because they cook so quickly, it is an easy and guilt-free pleasure to whip up for family and friends.

**PREP:** 10 minutes • **COOK:** 15 minutes • **SERVINGS:** 30

## Ingredients

¼ **cup cake flour (or all-purpose flour), sifted**

**3 tablespoons sugar**

**3 egg whites**

¼ **teaspoon vanilla extract**

**pinch salt**

¼ **teaspoon cream of tartar**

**2 teaspoons lime zest**

**3 teaspoons lime juice**

**2 cups water**

**4 tablespoons powdered sugar**

**1 kiwi, peeled, thinly sliced, and cut into quarters (pie-shaped)**

## Directions

1. In a small bowl, combine cake flour with 1 tablespoon sugar.

2. With an electric mixer set to high, beat egg whites, vanilla extract, salt, and cream of tartar until soft peaks form. Add 1 teaspoon lime zest and 1 teaspoon lime juice. Gradually add remaining 2 tablespoons sugar. Beat on high until mixture is fully incorporated, glossy, and stiff peaks are formed.

3. Fold in by hand flour and sugar mixture in thirds until fully incorporated, keeping batter as voluminous as possible.

4. Fill silicone mini-muffin tray with 1 tablespoon batter in each cup. Pour water into pot. Place rack in pot and tray on rack. Set OVEN to 325°F for 15 minutes, checking after 12 minutes, and cook until cupcakes rise and a toothpick inserted in centers comes out clean. Remove mini cupcakes and let cool.

5. Stir together remaining lime zest, 2 teaspoons lime juice, and powdered sugar and frost the tops of the cakes. Top with kiwi.

**NINJA** SERVING TIP

Cake flour will create a delicate, tender crumb, but all-purpose flour will work if that is what you have.

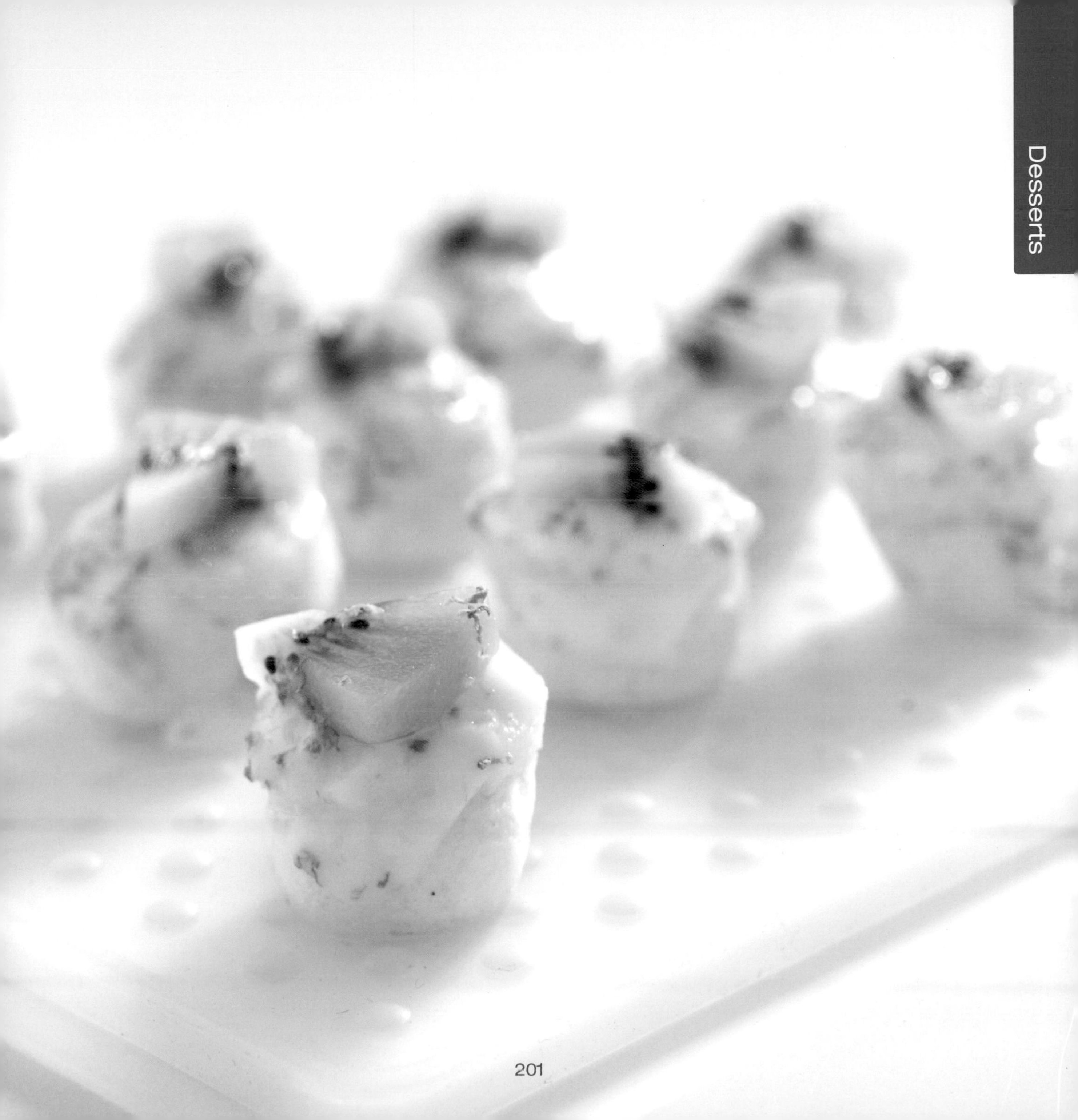

 STEAM OVEN

Desserts

# DULCE DE LECHE CAKE

This simplified version of the Latin American "Tres Leches" cake is drenched in cooked milk, steam baked to keep it moist, and served with plenty of fruit.

**PREP:** 10 minutes • **COOK:** 30 minutes  **CHILL:** 4 hours • **SERVINGS:** 8

## Ingredients

**1 package (15.25 ounces) yellow butter cake mix**

**4 cups water**

**½ cup caramel sauce**

**½ cup heavy cream**

**2 cups mixed fresh berries (strawberries, raspberries, blueberries)**

**whipped cream**

## Directions

**1.** Prepare cake mix batter according to package directions. Pour batter into multi-purpose pan.

**2.** Pour water into pot. Place rack into pot and place multi-purpose pan on rack. Set OVEN to 350°F for 30 minutes. Cover and cook until toothpick inserted in center comes out clean; remove pan and rack from pot and empty water.

**3.** Add caramel sauce and heavy cream to pot. Set to STOVETOP LOW. Stir constantly until sauce is warmed and fully incorporated. Keep sauce warm.

**4.** Poke holes all over cake using a straw or skewer, making sure to poke through to bottom of cake. Pour warm caramel mixture slowly all over cake so that it soaks into cake. Refrigerate cake 4 hours or overnight. Serve with berries and whipped cream.

**NINJA** HEALTHY TIP

You can follow reduced-fat directions on cake mix package to prepare cake batter, if you prefer.

 STEAM OVEN

# DOUBLE-CHOCOLATE ZUCCHINI MUFFINS

These chocolaty muffins have a secret ingredient: shredded zucchini! Not only does it add good-for-you fiber, but the zucchini helps keep the muffins moist as they bake up light and tender in the pot.

**PREP:** 5 minutes • **COOK:** 25 minutes • **SERVINGS:** 6

## Ingredients

1 package (6.5 ounces) chocolate chip muffin mix

2 tablespoons unsweetened cocoa powder

½ teaspoon ground cinnamon

1 medium zucchini, shredded

¼ cup water plus 2 cups water

½ teaspoon vanilla extract

## Directions

**1.** Line 6-cup muffin pan with paper liners.

**2.** Stir muffin mix, cocoa powder, and cinnamon in bowl. Stir in zucchini. Add ¼ cup water and vanilla extract and stir just until combined. Spoon batter into muffin pan cups, filling about ⅔ full.

**3.** Pour 2 cups water into pot. Place rack into pot. Place muffin pan on rack. Set OVEN to 375°F for 25 minutes. Cover and cook until wooden pick inserted in centers comes out clean. Immediately remove muffins from pan and let cool on cooling rack 10 minutes.

 SERVING TIP

Serve with seedless raspberry jam for spreading.

 STEAM OVEN

# SALTED CARAMEL DEVIL'S FOOD MINI CUPCAKES

**Fleur de sel is a special salt with an earthy, delicious flavor that perfectly complements the sweet caramel-cheese frosting.**

**PREP:** 20 minutes • **COOK:** 11 minutes • **SERVINGS:** 36

## Ingredients

**1 cup flour**

**⅓ cup unsweetened cocoa**

**1 teaspoon baking soda**

**salt**

**⅔ cup sugar**

**¼ cup butter, softened**

**½ cup egg substitute**

**1 teaspoon vanilla**

**½ cup skim milk**

**1¼ ounces semi-sweet chocolate, finely chopped**

**1½ cups water**

**⅓ of an 8-ounce package fat-free cream cheese**

**⅓ of an 8-ounce fat-free whipped topping**

**2 tablespoons plus 2 teaspoons caramel sauce, fat-free**

## Directions

**1.** In a small bowl, sift together the flour, cocoa, baking soda, and salt.

**2.** Beat sugar and butter in a bowl at medium speed until combined. Add egg and vanilla, beating well. Add flour mixture and milk alternately to sugar butter mixture, until combined. Fold in chopped chocolate.

**3.** Add batter into silicone petite muffin tray. Place the rack in pot and set the pan on the rack. Add water to the pot. Set OVEN to 350°F for 15 minutes, checking after 10 minutes. Cover and cook until a toothpick inserted in center comes out clean. Remove tray and let cool.

**4.** Beat cream cheese and caramel in a mixing bowl until soft. Add whipped topping and gently fold in, scraping down sides till combined. Top each cupcake with 2 teaspoons frosting, drizzle of fat-free caramel sauce (optional), and a pinch of fleur de sel.

**NINJA** TIME-SAVER TIP

Melt the butter and the chocolate together to save a step.

 **OVEN**

# S'MORES BREAD PUDDING

You do not have to sit around a campfire to enjoy this dessert, but it might earn you a badge.

**PREP:** 15 minutes • **COOK:** 50 minutes • **SERVINGS:** 6–8

## Ingredients

**4 cups cubed challah bread**

**1 cup mini marshmallows**

**¾ cup semi-sweet morsels**

**8 graham cracker squares, crushed**

**4 large eggs**

**¼ teaspoon cinnamon**

**1 teaspoon vanilla extract**

**1 cup milk**

**1 can (14 ounces) sweetened condensed milk**

## Directions

**1.** Set OVEN to 350°F. Spray multi-purpose pan with baking spray.

**2.** Place half of the cubed bread in multi-purpose pan and top bread with half of the marshmallows, semi-sweet morsels, and graham cracker crumbs. Repeat layers.

**3.** Whisk together eggs, cinnamon, vanilla, milk, and condensed milk. Pour over bread mixture. Press down mixture to help bread absorb the liquid.

**4.** Place multi-purpose pan rack in pot and place multi-purpose pan on rack. Set timer for 50 minutes.

**5.** Remove pan and serve immediately.

**NINJA** SERVING TIP

Use any old leftover bread in this bread pudding. Kids love to help build the layers in the pan; that way they can sneak a few morsels and marshmallows.

 STOVETOP/OVEN

# CARAMEL PEAR CRUMBLE

This "upside down" crumble allows the butter and sugar to melt on the bottom, creating a caramel coating with the oats. A delicious dessert recipe with ice cream, or a brunch delight!

**PREP:** 10 minutes • **COOK:** 1½ hours • **SERVINGS:** 6–8

## Ingredients

¾ cup old-fashioned oats

½ cup packed brown sugar

⅓ cup flour plus 2 teaspoons

½ teaspoon ground cinnamon (for caramel oat layer) plus ½ teaspoon ground cinnamon (for fruit)

¼ teaspoon kosher salt

¾ stick (6 tablespoons) unsalted butter, room temperature

6 large pears, peeled, cored into thin slices

¼ cup sugar

1 tablespoon lemon juice

1 tablespoon vanilla extract

## Directions

1. Grease a standard loaf pan with light butter or cooking spray.

2. In a medium bowl, add oats, brown sugar, ⅓ cup flour, ½ teaspoon cinnamon, and salt. Add butter and combine with a fork and fingertips to incorporate mixture into smaller pea-sized pieces, or a food processor.

3. Combine pears, sugar, juice, 2 teaspoons flour and ½ teaspoon cinnamon in a large bowl. Spread loaf pan with oat mixture and top with pear mixture; cover with foil. Place loaf pan on rack. Set OVEN to 425°F for 1 hour.

4. Remove foil, cover, and set OVEN to 350°F for 30 minutes and cook until pears are softened. Let cool and serve with vanilla ice cream if desired.

**NINJA** SERVING TIP

Serve with a dollop of whipped cream with brown sugar sprinkled on top.

 OVEN

# PEACH ALMOND COBBLER WITH COOKIE TOPPING

**Frozen peaches make the prep easy in this recipe. The reserved juices thicken in the pot to make a delicious cobbler filling topped with crunchy cookie crumbs.**

**PREP:** 10 minutes • **COOK:** 30 minutes • **SERVINGS:** 8

## Ingredients

**4 bags (16 ounces each) frozen sliced peaches, thawed and drained, juice reserved**

**2 tablespoons cornstarch**

**½ cup sugar**

**2 teaspoons almond extract**

**1 package (7 ounces) almond or sugar cookies, crushed (about 2 cups crushed)**

**sweetened whipped cream**

## Directions

**1.** Stir reserved peach juice and cornstarch in pot. Add peaches, sugar, and almond extract and stir to coat. Set OVEN to 325°F for 30 minutes. Cover and bake until peaches are tender.

**2.** Turn off pot. Let peach mixture cool in pot 5 minutes. Sprinkle with cookie crumbs. Serve with whipped cream.

**NINJA** HEALTHY TIP

For a healthful twist, try using your favorite granola or chopped toasted almonds instead of almond cookies.

Desserts

# CHOCOLATE TIRAMISU-FILLED CUPCAKES

The cupcake is soft and spongy like a ladyfinger, only mocha-flavored. Once you dust with the cocoa powder, you have just put tiramisu into the hands of six lucky people.

**PREP:** 20 minutes • **COOK:** 20 minutes • **SERVINGS:** 6

## Ingredients

**2 cups water**

**½ cup all-purpose flour**

**½ cup sugar**

**1 tablespoon cocoa powder**

**¼ teaspoon baking soda**

**⅛ teaspoon salt**

**¼ cup milk**

**1 tablespoon espresso powder**

**1 large egg**

**½ teaspoon coffee extract**

**½ teaspoon vanilla extract**

**8 ounces cream cheese, softened**

**8 ounces mascarpone cheese, softened**

**½ cup confectioners' sugar**

**1 teaspoon vanilla extract**

## Directions

**1.** Spray six freestanding silicone cupcake liners with baking spray and place in multi-purpose pan on rack.

**2.** Whisk together flour, sugar, cocoa powder, baking soda, and salt in a large bowl. In a separate bowl, whisk espresso powder into milk. Once dissolved, whisk in egg and ½ teaspoon each coffee and vanilla extracts.

**3.** Stir liquid ingredients into dry and divide cake mixture between six cupcake liners. Set OVEN to 350°F and add water. Place pan onto rack in pot, cover, set timer for 20 minutes, and bake. Meanwhile, beat together cream cheese and mascarpone cheese until smooth for icing. Add confectioners' sugar and vanilla and beat until smooth.

**4.** Turn pot off. Remove pan from pot and place on rack. Let cupcakes cool completely. Remove center with an apple corer once cooled.

**5.** Fill pastry bag with icing. Put on a medium round tip. Pipe icing into center hole and swirl icing over top of cupcake. Dust with cocoa powder.

**NINJA** SERVING TIP

This recipe makes extra icing, but I use it to stuff strawberries for a quick dessert.

 **STEAM OVEN**

# CAPPUCCINO MOLTEN LAVA CAKES

Take the guesswork out of baking molten chocolate cakes. The efficient heating in the pot bakes the outsides to perfection leaving a gooey chocolate-coffee center.

**PREP:** 5 minutes • **COOK:** 20 minutes • **SERVINGS:** 6

## Ingredients

**cooking spray**

**1 cup semi-sweet chocolate chips, melted**

**½ cup butter, melted**

**1 cup confectioners' sugar**

**2 eggs**

**2 egg yolks**

**2 tablespoons coffee-flavored liqueur**

**1 teaspoon vanilla extract**

**½ cup flour**

**2 cups water**

## Directions

1. Spray 6-cup muffin pan with cooking spray. Line bottoms of muffin pan cups with waxed paper circles and spray with cooking spray.

2. In a medium bowl, add chocolate and butter and stir until smooth. Stir in sugars. Stir in eggs and egg yolks. Stir in liqueur, vanilla extract, and flour. Spoon batter into muffin pan cups.

3. Pour water into pot. Place rack into pot. Place pan on rack. Set OVEN to 425°F for 20 minutes. Cover and cook until sides of cakes are firm but centers are still soft. Remove pan from pot and let stand 2 minutes. Run knife around sides of cakes to loosen. Invert onto serving plate. Serve warm.

**NINJA** SERVING TIP

Serve with whipped cream dusted with cinnamon. Try different flavors by substituting raspberry or hazelnut liqueur for the coffee-flavored liqueur.

FRITTATA WITH HASH BROWNS & BACON

# CHAPTER 9:
# Breakfasts

STEAM OVEN

# BLUEBERRY PANCAKE MUFFINS

Buttermilk blueberry pancakes — in a muffin! These quick-to-make muffins bake up light and moist in the pot, thanks to the steam-baking technique.

**PREP:** 15 minutes • **COOK:** 25 minutes • **SERVINGS:** 6

## Ingredients

1 cup all-purpose flour

1½ teaspoons baking powder

¼ teaspoon baking soda

¼ teaspoon salt

2 teaspoons sugar

¾ cup buttermilk

1 tablespoon canola oil

1 egg

3 tablespoons canned blueberries, drained

cooking spray

1½ cups hot water

## Directions

1. Stir flour, baking powder, baking soda, salt, and sugar in bowl.

2. Beat buttermilk, oil, and egg in another bowl. Add buttermilk mixture to flour mixture and stir just until combined. Stir in blueberries.

3. Spray 6-cup muffin pan with cooking spray. Spoon batter into muffin-pan cups.

4. Pour water into pot. Place rack into pot. Place pan on rack. Set OVEN to 350°F for 25 minutes. Cover and cook until wooden pick inserted in centers comes out clean.

**NINJA** SERVING TIP

Sprinkle with confectioners' sugar and serve with maple butter.

**STOVETOP/SLOW COOK**

# MAPLE CINNAMON OATMEAL

**Breakfast oatmeal should be prepared the night before, so it can slow cook on low while you are sleeping.**

**PREP:** 15 minutes • **COOK:** 6–8 hours • **SERVINGS:** 4

## Ingredients

**4 cups low-fat milk**

**4 tablespoons pure maple syrup**

**2 tablespoons butter, cut up**

**2 teaspoons vanilla extract**

**1 teaspoon ground cinnamon**

**¼ teaspoon ground nutmeg**

**pinch salt**

**1 cup uncooked steel-cut oats**

**1 cup dried cherries**

## Directions

**1.** Stir milk, syrup, butter, vanilla extract, cinnamon, nutmeg, and salt in pot. Set to STOVETOP HIGH. Cover and cook 10 minutes or until butter is melted.

**2.** Stir in oats. Set to SLOW COOK LOW for 6–8 hours. Cover and cook until oats are tender and mixture is creamy. Stir in cherries.

**NINJA** SERVING TIP

Try adding cut-up bananas, apples, pears, or raisins. For creamier oatmeal, stir in a touch of milk with each serving.

 **STOVETOP**

# FRITTATA WITH HASH BROWN POTATOES & BACON

This Italian omelet is loaded with peppers, potatoes, bacon, and cheese. Cook everything in the pot — then stir in the eggs and cover to finish cooking — the frittata stays moist and delicious.

**PREP:** 15 minutes • **COOK:** 30 minutes • **SERVINGS:** 6

## Ingredients

2 tablespoons canola oil

1 large onion, chopped

1 large green pepper, chopped

4 strips turkey bacon, chopped

½ of a 32-ounce package frozen diced hash brown potatoes (about 3½ cups)

12 eggs

¾ cup low-fat milk

½ teaspoon salt

¼ teaspoon ground black pepper

1 cup shredded low-fat Cheddar cheese

## Directions

1. Pour oil into pot. Set to STOVETOP HIGH and heat oil. Add onion, green pepper, and bacon to pot. Cook uncovered 15 minutes or until vegetables are tender, stirring often.

2. Stir in potatoes. Cover and cook 5 minutes.

3. Beat eggs, milk, salt, and black pepper in bowl. Set pot to STOVETOP LOW. Stir egg mixture and cheese into pot. Cover and cook 10 minutes or until the egg mixture is set.

**NINJA** SERVING TIP

Serve topped with additional chopped cooked bacon, if desired.

STOVETOP/OVEN

# VEGETABLE FRITTATA

Lots of fresh vegetables and a surprise of sweet potatoes make this frittata an original!

**PREP:** 15 minutes • **COOK:** 30–34 minutes • **SERVINGS:** 4–6

## Ingredients

2 tablespoons olive oil

1 medium onion, chopped

1 red pepper, diced

1 medium sweet potato, diced

2 cups baby spinach

8 large eggs

1 cup milk

salt and pepper to taste

2 cups broccoli florets

1 cup shredded Cheddar cheese

## Directions

1. Set pot to STOVETOP HIGH and add oil. Add onion, red pepper, and sweet potatoes. Stir once, cover, and cook 4 minutes.

2. Add spinach and broccoli to pot and sauté 1 minute to wilt, stirring the whole time. Remove cooked vegetables and keep warm.

3. Whisk together eggs and milk and season with salt and pepper. Add cooked vegetable and Cheddar cheese. Carefully pour egg mixture into pot, and set OVEN to 350°F. Bake for 30 minutes.

4. Remove roasting pan from pot and divide frittata among four to six plates. Serve immediately.

**NINJA** SERVING TIP

Not into sweet potatoes? Try Yukon Golds.

**STOVETOP/SLOW COOK**

# APPLE FRENCH TOAST CASSEROLE

This warm bread pudding is perfect for a special breakfast or brunch. Apples and pecans cook in the pot with a maple-butter sauce, then are tossed with cubes of challah in a spiced milk mixture. Cover and let the sweet aroma fill your kitchen as it cooks.

**PREP:** 20 minutes • **COOK:** 2 hours, 10 minutes • **SERVINGS:** 6

## Ingredients

½ **cup butter**

2 **Granny Smith apples, peeled, cored, and chopped**

1 **cup chopped pecans**

½ **cup packed brown sugar**

½ **cup pure maple syrup**

1 **loaf challah bread (about 1 pound), cut into cubes**

6 **large eggs**

2 **cups milk**

2 **teaspoons ground cinnamon**

1 **tablespoon vanilla extract**

**pinch salt**

**confectioners' sugar**

## Directions

**1.** Place butter into pot. Set to STOVETOP HIGH and heat until butter is melted. Place apples, pecans, brown sugar, and syrup in pot. Cook uncovered 10 minutes or until apples are tender, stirring often.

**2.** Place bread in bowl. Beat eggs, milk, cinnamon, vanilla extract, and salt in another bowl. Pour egg mixture over bread and stir to coat. Pour bread mixture into pot and stir. Set to SLOW COOK HIGH for 2–3 hours. Cover and cook until center is set. Turn off pot. Let stand 10 minutes before serving. Sprinkle with confectioners' sugar.

**NINJA** HEALTHY TIP

Use refrigerated egg substitute in place of eggs and 1% milk instead of whole as a healthier swap of ingredients.

**STOVETOP**

# BROCCOLI CHEESE SCRAMBLED EGGS

Simply cook the broccoli in the pot, add the eggs and tangy shredded Cheddar, and breakfast is ready — in 15 minutes!

**PREP:** 5 minutes • **COOK:** 12 minutes • **SERVINGS:** 4

## Ingredients

**1 package (12 ounces) frozen broccoli florets**

**2 tablespoons butter**

**salt and ground black pepper**

**8 eggs**

**2 tablespoons low-fat milk**

**¾ cup shredded low-fat white Cheddar cheese**

**crushed red pepper (optional)**

## Directions

**1.** Place broccoli and butter into pot and season with salt and black pepper. Set to STOVETOP HIGH. Cover and cook 10 minutes or until broccoli is tender, stirring occasionally.

**2.** Beat eggs and milk in bowl. Stir egg mixture in pot. Set to STOVETOP LOW and cook uncovered 2 minutes or until egg mixture is set, stirring often. Stir in cheese. Season with salt, black pepper, and red pepper, if desired.

**NINJA** HEALTHY TIP

Substitute egg whites for half the eggs and omit cheese.

 STEAM OVEN

# LOW-FAT SPICED MAPLE CORN MUFFINS

Start with a box of packaged corn muffin mix, then spice it up with maple syrup and cinnamon for a new favorite breakfast treat. The pot insulates as it bakes, which means that your corn muffins are always moist.

**PREP:** 5 minutes • **COOK:** 15 minutes • **SERVINGS:** 6

## Ingredients

**cooking spray**

**1 package (6.5 ounces) corn bread and muffin mix**

**2 egg whites**

**¼ cup fat-free milk**

**¼ cup pure maple syrup**

**1 teaspoon ground cinnamon**

**2 cups water**

## Directions

**1.** Spray 6-cup muffin pan with cooking spray.

**2.** Stir muffin mix, egg whites, milk, syrup, and cinnamon in bowl. Spoon batter into muffin-pan cups.

**3.** Pour water into pot. Place rack into pot. Place pan onto rack. Set OVEN to 400°F for 15 minutes. Cover and bake until wooden pick inserted in centers comes out clean.

**NINJA** SERVING TIP

Serve with your favorite fruit butter, like apple butter or pumpkin butter.

 **STOVETOP**

# GRITS SOUTHERN STYLE

Cooking the onions and bacon in the maple syrup candies them. When you stir them back into the dish at the end, you get a sweet and smoky cheese breakfast treat that cannot be beat.

**PREP:** 5 minutes • **COOK:** 28–35 minutes • **SERVINGS:** 4

## Ingredients

½ medium yellow onions, finely diced

3 slices thick-cut bacon, finely diced

3 tablespoons pure maple syrup

4 cups water

1 cup white corn grits

¼ teaspoon salt

1 cup low-fat sharp Cheddar cheese, shredded

## Directions

**1.** Set pot to STOVETOP HIGH. Add onion and bacon and sauté 8–10 minutes, stirring occasionally.

**2.** Add maple syrup and cook 5 minutes, stirring occasionally. Remove bacon and onion and keep warm.

**3.** Add water, cover with lid, and bring to a boil. Add grits slowly, stirring the whole time. Stir in salt.

**4.** Set pot to STOVETOP LOW, cover, and cook 15–20 minutes, stirring occasionally.

**5.** Add Cheddar cheese and bacon and onion mixture, stir to melt cheese and blend ingredients, then serve immediately.

**NINJA** SERVING TIP

For a richer bowl of grits, stir in some heavy cream; for sweeter, stir in some more maple syrup.

**STOVETOP/SLOW COOK**

# TURKEY SAUSAGE, EGG, & CHEESE STRATA

This one-pot breakfast features eggs, sausage, tomatoes, cheese, and bread for a hearty start to your day and is especially great for weekend brunch.

**PREP:** 20 minutes • **COOK:** 2 hours, 20 minutes • **SERVINGS:** 6

## Ingredients

1 tablespoon canola oil

1¼ pounds turkey sausage, casing removed

1 medium onion, chopped

1 tablespoon chopped garlic

2 medium plum tomatoes, chopped

1 tablespoon dried basil leaves, crushed

10 eggs, beaten

2 cups milk

5 cups sliced Italian bread cut into ½-inch pieces

1 cup shredded Monterey Jack cheese

salt and ground black pepper

**NINJA** SERVING TIP

For a spicy dish, use hot Italian sausage instead of turkey sausage.

## Directions

**1.** Pour oil into pot. Set to STOVETOP HIGH and heat oil. Add sausage to pot. Cook uncovered 10 minutes or until sausage is cooked through, stirring occasionally. Remove sausage from pot.

**2.** Stir onion, garlic, tomatoes, and basil in pot. Cook uncovered 5 minutes or until onion is tender, stirring occasionally. Remove vegetable mixture from pot.

**3.** Stir eggs, milk, bread, cheese, salt, and black pepper in bowl. Stir in sausage and vegetable mixture. Pour egg mixture into pot. Set to SLOW COOK HIGH for 2–3 hours. Cover and cook until mixture is set.

 STOVETOP

# STEEL-CUT OATMEAL

Of the various forms of hot oat cereals, steel-cut oats are the least processed and as a result have a chewier, denser texture. They also keep you fuller and satisfied longer than those instant or quick-cooking oatmeal.

**PREP:** 5 minutes • **COOK:** 25–30 minutes • **SERVINGS:** 4

## Ingredients

**4 cups water**

**1 cup steel-cut oatmeal**

**¼ teaspoon salt**

**¼ teaspoon ground cinnamon**

**¼ cup golden raisins**

**¼ cup chopped pecans**

## Directions

**1.** Add water to pot and set to STOVETOP HIGH. Cover with lid, and bring to a boil.

**2.** Add steel-cut oatmeal, salt, and ground cinnamon, then stir gently.

**3.** Set pot to STOVETOP LOW, remove lid, and cook 25–30 minutes.

**4.** Stir in dried cherries and chopped pecans. Serve immediately.

**NINJA** SERVING TIP

If you want to infuse your oatmeal with the flavor of the fruit, add it at the beginning.

 **STOVETOP**

# CORNED BEEF HASH BREAKFAST

This updated version of corned beef hash features chopped corned beef stirred into eggs scrambled with sour cream. The potatoes are hash brown patties that are cooked from frozen right in the pot, then served as a side dish. Breakfast is served!

**PREP:** 10 minutes • **COOK:** 20 minutes • **SERVINGS:** 4

## Ingredients

2 tablespoons butter

4 frozen hash brown potato patties

¼ pound sliced corned beef, chopped

4 eggs

½ cup sour cream

¼ cup chopped green onions

salt and ground black pepper

## Directions

1. Place butter into pot. Set to STOVETOP HIGH and heat until butter is melted. Add potato patties to pot. Cook uncovered 10 minutes or until crisp on both sides. Remove potato patties from pot and keep warm.

2. Place corned beef into pot. Cook 1 minute or until hot.

3. Stir eggs, sour cream, green onions, salt, and black pepper in bowl. Stir egg mixture into pot. Cover and cook 4 minutes or until eggs are set. Serve patties with egg mixture.

**NINJA** SERVING TIP

Serve with sliced fresh tomatoes or fresh mixed fruit.

STOVETOP/OVEN

# SPRING FRITTATA

Eggs are the least expensive protein but can be a satisfying meal, and not just breakfast!

**PREP:** 10 minutes • **COOK:** 30 minutes • **SERVINGS:** 8

## Ingredients

**12 eggs**

**salt and ground black pepper**

**2 tablespoons butter**

**1 tablespoon canola oil**

**1 large onion, thinly sliced**

**1 tablespoon chopped fresh thyme leaves**

**1 cup asparagus tips, cooked**

**1 small cooked potato, cut into ¼-inch slices**

**1½ cups grated Gruyère cheese**

**chopped fresh chives**

## Directions

1. Beat eggs in bowl. Season with salt and black pepper.

2. Place butter and oil into the pot. Set to STOVETOP HIGH and heat until butter is melted. Add thyme and onion to pot and season with salt and black pepper. Cook uncovered 20 minutes or until onions are deep brown and tender, stirring occasionally.

3. Stir eggs in pot. Cook 1 minute. Stir in asparagus, potato, and cheese. Set to OVEN to 325°F for 10 minutes. After 3 minutes, gently stir mixture to get uncooked eggs to bottom of pot. Cover and cook until egg mixture is set.

4. Invert frittata onto serving platter. Sprinkle with chives.

## NINJA SERVING TIP

If chives are not available, either chopped scallions or chopped parsley will serve as a good alternative.

 **STEAM OVEN**

# HOLIDAY APPLE SPICE CAKE

This delicious cake is light enough for holiday brunches, or serve it with vanilla ice cream as a dessert!

**PREP:** 15 minutes • **COOK:** 40 minutes • **SERVINGS:** 10–12

## Ingredients

2 tablespoons maple syrup

1 Honeycrisp apple, peeled, cored, and sliced very thin

1 cup all-purpose flour

½ teaspoon cinnamon

¼ teaspoon allspice

¼ teaspoon ginger

½ teaspoon baking soda

½ teaspoon baking powder

½ teaspoon salt

6 tablespoons unsalted butter, softened

¾ cup granulated sugar

2 eggs

1 teaspoon vanilla

½ cup buttermilk

## Directions

1. Spray the inside of a loaf pan with nonstick spray and pour maple syrup over the bottom, coating evenly. Arrange apple slices along the bottom of the pan with some overlapping to create a scale pattern.

2. In a medium bowl, sift together flour, cinnamon, allspice, ginger, baking soda, baking powder, and salt.

3. In a large bowl, use an electric mixer at medium-high speed to mix the butter and sugar 5 minutes until light and fluffy.

4. Add eggs to the butter and sugar mixture one at a time, mixing well after each addition. Add vanilla. Reduce speed to low and alternate adding the flour mixture and the buttermilk in batches until fully blended. Spoon batter into loaf pan and smooth the top.

5. Pour 4 cups water into the pot and place the loaf pan on the rack. Set OVEN to 350℉ and bake until a toothpick comes out clean, about 40 minutes.

6. Cool cake in pan on a rack 10 minutes and invert onto plate before serving.

**NINJA** HEALTHY TIP

Substitute whole-grain flour and "lite" maple syrup.

NINJA
COOKING SYSTEM
SLOW COOK
LOW
HIGH
OFF
STOVETOP
LOW
HIGH
OVEN
BAKE / ROAST
STEAMER
10:30
TIME / OVEN TEMP
POWER
AUTO WARM

# CHAPTER 10:
## Charts & Index

# Steam-Infused Roasting

| | | Cooking Infusions | | |
|---|---|---|---|---|
| Protein | Flavor Choice | Liquid | Seasoning | Extra Flavor Ingredients |
| CHICKEN<br><br>*1 hour cooktime for 3-4 lbs.*<br>*Steam Oven at 375°F* | Tuscan | 3 cups White Wine, ½ cup Lemon Juice | 1 cup Arugula | 1 cup Fennel, 1 cup Pear |
| | Mediterranean | 4 cups Chicken Broth | 2 tsp. dried Oregano | ½ cup Feta Cheese |
| | Caribbean | 2 cups Orange Juice, 2 cups Broth | 1 cup Onion, 2 cups Bell Pepper | 2 Tb. Cumin, 1 cup Cilantro |
| | Thai | 2 cans Coconut Milk, ½ cup Water | 1½ Tb. minced Ginger | ¼ cup Curry Paste |
| FISH<br><br>*30 minutes cooktime for 2 lbs.*<br>*Steam Oven at 350°F* | Southern | 2 cups Fish Stock | ½ cup Onion | ½ cup Bacon, 1 cup Corn |
| | French | 2 cups White Wine | 1 cup Leek | 1 cup Mushrooms |
| | Italian | 2 cups Broth | 2 tsp. dried Basil, 2 minced Garlic Cloves | 1 can Cannellini Beans undrained, ½ pkg. frozen Spinach |
| | Lemon Dill | 1½ cups Wine, ½ cup Lemon Juice | 1 Tb. chopped Dill | 1 Tb. Dijon Mustard |
| PORK<br><br>*40 minutes cooktime for 2-3 lbs.*<br>*Steam Oven at 375°F* | German | 4 cups Chicken Broth | 2 minced Garlic Cloves, 1 tsp. Allspice | 2 cups Onion |
| | Sweet/Savory | 4 cups Apple Juice | 1 cup Onion | 4 cups Red Cabbage |
| | American | 2 cups Broth, 2 cups Barbecue Sauce | 2 minced Garlic Cloves | ½ cup Bacon |
| | French | 4 cups Chicken Broth | 4 Cloves | ¼ cup Honey Mustard |
| BEEF<br><br>*40 minutes cooktime for 2-3 lbs.*<br>*Steam Oven at 350°F* | Mexican | 2 cups Salsa, 2 cups Beef Broth | 2 Tb. chopped Chilies, 2 tsp. Cumin | 2 minced Garlic Cloves, ½ cup Cilantro |
| | Asian | 2 cups Teriyaki Sauce, 2 cups Water | ½ cup Green Onions, 4 minced Garlic Cloves | ½ Tb. minced Ginger, 2 Tb. Hot Garlic Paste |
| | Greek | 3 cups Red Wine, 1 cup Water | 1 can Tomato Paste, 2 Tb. Olive Oil | 2 Tb. chopped Rosemary |
| | Spain | 1 can diced Tomatoes, 2 cups Chicken Broth | 2 cups Red Bell Pepper, 4 minced Garlic Cloves | 1 cup Sherry, 2 tsp. Saffron |

# Steam Roast Flavor Substitutes

Have fun with the recipes and take something from ordinary to extraordinary with the quick change of a rub, sauce, flavorful infusion, crispy crust, or warm topping. Try out some of the recommendations below to change up one of your favorites or create a new one!

| Flavor Substitutes | | | |
|---|---|---|---|
| **Rubs** | **Sauces & Glazes** | **Crispy Crust** | **Hot Warm Crust** |
| Whether you are Sear/Cooking, Steam or Oven Roasting, these rubs will definitely kick your meal up a notch. | Baste your meat or fish with these sauces for an extra kick 15–30 minutes before they are done cooking when using your ROAST mode. | Pre-crisp in the STOVETOP HIGH setting till golden brown, then just sprinkle over cooked meats, fish, or vegetables. | Place on meat or vegetables 5 minutes before cooking is done. |
| Lemon Pepper Seasoning | Barbecue Sauce | Ritz, Butter, Parsley | Blue Cheese, Honey |
| Cajun Seasoning | Southwest Barbecue (blended with Chipotle in Adobo Purée, cumin, and lime juice) | Panko, Butter, Italian Seasoning, Parmesan | Gorgonzola, Walnut |
| Montreal Seasoning | | Panko, Hazelnut, Butter, | Fontina, Garlic, |
| Peppercorn | | Salt, Pepper | Sautéed Spinach |
| Asian Five-Spice Seasoning & Orange Peel | Korean Barbecue | Sesame (Black and White) | Country Dijon Herb |
| Garlic, Parsley, Parmesan | Hoisin | Almond, Parsley, Lemon Peel | Pesto |
| Dijon Herb (Try Parsley, Herb de Provence, or Rosemary) | Sweet Chili Sauce | Za'tar, Pistachio | |
| | | Coconut, Macadamia Nut | |
| | | Panko, Coconut, Cayenne | |

# Slow Cooker Cooking Guide

## Beef

| Type of Beef | Cook Time LOW | Cook Time HIGH |
|---|---|---|
| Top Round | 8–10 hours | 4–5 hours |
| Bottom Round | 8–10 hours | 4–5 hours |
| Chuck | 8–10 hours | 4–5 hours |
| Stew Meat (Beef, Lamb, Veal, Rabbit) | 7–9 hours | 3–4 hours |
| Eye of the Round, Sirloin | 6–8 hours | 3–4 hours |
| Short Ribs | 7–9 hours | 3½–4½ hours |
| Brisket | 7–9 hours | 3½–4½ hours |
| Pot Roast | 7–9 hours | 3½–4½ hours |
| Frozen Meatballs (precooked) | 6–8 hours | 3–4 hours |

## Pork

| Type of Pork | Cook Time LOW | Cook Time HIGH |
|---|---|---|
| Baby Back Ribs | 7–9 hours | 3½–4½ hours |
| Country Ribs | 7–9 hours | 3½–4½ hours |
| Pork Tenderloin | 6–7 hours | 3–4 hours |
| Pork Loin | 7–9 hours | 3½–4½ hours |
| Pork Rib Roast | 7–9 hours | 3½–4½ hours |
| Pork Butt | 10–12 hours | 5–6 hours |
| Pork Shoulder | 10–12 hours | 5–6 hours |
| Ham (fully cooked) | 5–7 hours | 2½–3½ hours |
| Ham, Bone-In (uncooked) | 7–9 hours | 3½–4½ hours |

# Slow Cooker Cooking Guide

| Poultry | | |
| --- | --- | --- |
| **Type of Poultry** | **Cook Time LOW** | **Cook Time HIGH** |
| Boneless, Skinless Breast | 6–7 hours | 3–4 hours |
| Boneless, Skinless Thighs | 6–7½ hours | 3–4½ hours |
| Bone-In Breast | 6–7½ hours | 3–4½ hours |
| Bone-In Thighs | 7–9 hours | 3½–4½ hours |
| Whole Chicken | 7–9 hours | 3½–4½ hours |
| Chicken Wings | 6–7 hours | 3–4 hours |
| Turkey Breast | 7–9 hours | 3½–4½ hours |
| Turkey Thighs | 7–9 hours | 3½–4½ hours |

| Fish | | |
| --- | --- | --- |
| **Type of Fish** | **Cook Time LOW** | **Cook Time HIGH** |
| 1-inch Fillets | --- | 30–45 minutes |
| Frozen Shrimp | Add during last 20–30 minutes of cooking | Add during last 20–30 minutes of cooking |
| Fresh Shellfish | Add during last 20–30 minutes of cooking | Add during last 20–30 minutes of cooking |

# Layered Meals

Prepare complete meals in a single pot on the OVEN setting by choosing a protein, a vegetable, and a starch from the chart below and layering them in the pot to cook together at the same time. Thicker protein and vegetables will require slightly longer cook times; adjust times as necessary. Layered Meal Instructions: Preheat OVEN to 350°F and layer starch on the bottom of the pot with recommended amount of water per the package cooking instructions. Insert the rack and lay protein and vegetables on rack. Close lid and bake according to chart below.

## Quick Cooking (9 Minutes or Less)

| Protein | Vegetable | Starch |
|---|---|---|
| Fish Fillets | Thin Asparagus and Thin Zucchini | Couscous |
| Small Chicken Cutlets | Bell Peppers | 90-Second Microwave Rice |
| Frozen Shrimp/Frozen Fish Fillets | Haricots Verts | Israeli Couscous |
| | Spinach | Kasha |
| | Onions and Mushrooms | 5-Minute Long-Grain |
| | Pea Pods or Sugar Snap Peas | Wild Rice |
| | Frozen Peas | |

## Medium Cooking (10–20 Minutes)

| Protein | Vegetable | Starch |
|---|---|---|
| Frozen Large Chicken Cutlets | Broccoli | 10-Minute Quick Barley |
| Frozen Shrimp/Frozen Fish Fillets | Cauliflower | Farro |
| | Green Beans | Bulger |
| | Thick Asparagus | Quinoa |
| | Thick-Sliced Zucchini or Eggplant | 10-Minute Rice |

## Longer Cooking (20+ Minutes)

| Protein | Vegetable | Starch |
|---|---|---|
| Frozen Boneless Chicken Breast | Carrots | White Rice |
| Beef Roast (1½ inch or smaller | Sweet Potatoes | Jasmine Rice |
| if using steaming tray) | Parsnips or Turnips | Pilaf |
| Bone-In Meats, Chicken Thighs | Rutabagas | |
| | Artichokes | |
| | Corn on the Cob | |

# Pasta Cooking Chart — No Need to Drain!

For quick and easy pasta preparation that is ready in a snap without the time needed to boil and drain, look no further than your Ninja 4-in-1 Cooking System.

Simply follow the chart below, referring to the recommended cooking time on the box of the pasta. Find the cook time and amount of water needed to cook perfectly done pasta with no draining necessary.

Follow these directions:

Add the pasta, designated amount of water, 1–2 tablespoons butter, and 1 teaspoon of salt to the pot and gently stir to submerge pasta. Set OVEN to 250°F and set timer according to the chart below. Cook covered for 10 minutes, open, stir, cover, and cook for remaining time.

## Pasta Cooking Chart

| 1 Pound Box Recommended Cook Time | Water | Ninja Cook Time | Percentage of Time Saved with the Ninja* |
|---|---|---|---|
| 4 minutes | 2¾ cups | 10–12 minutes | 50% time savings |
| 7 minutes | 3 cups | 15–18 minutes | 33% time savings |
| 9 minutes | 3¼ cups | 20–22 minutes | 31% time savings |
| 11 minutes | 3½ cups | 20–22 minutes | 29% time savings |

* Time to boil water (approximately 20 minutes) plus pasta cooking time.

# Steamer Setting Chart

## Vegetable Steaming Chart

| Vegetable | Size/Preparation | Cooking Time | Liquid | Seasoning Ideas Salt & Pepper Plus: |
|---|---|---|---|---|
| Artichokes | whole | 25–40 minutes | 4 cups | olive oil, lemon zest |
| Asparagus | whole spears | 7–13 minutes | 3 cups | olive oil |
| Beans, green | whole | 6–10 minutes | 2 cups | garlic, minced |
| Beans, wax | whole | 6–10 minutes | 2 cups | Italian seasoning |
| Beets | whole, unpeeled | 35–50 minutes | 4 cups | garlic, minced |
| Beet greens | coarsely chopped | 7–9 minutes | 2 cups | thyme |
| Broccoli | trimmed stalks | 1–12 minutes | 3 cups | olive oil |
| Broccoli | florets | 5–7 minutes | 2 cups | olive oil |
| Brussels sprouts | whole, trimmed | 8–15 minutes | 3 cups | thyme |
| Cabbage | cut in wedges | 6–10 minutes | 2 cups | lemon juice |
| Carrots | ¼-inch slices | 7–10 minutes | 2 cups | maple syrup |
| Carrots, baby | whole baby carrots | 7–10 minutes | 2 cups | honey and ginger |
| Cauliflower | florets | 5–10 minutes | 2 cups | lemon juice |
| Celery stalks | ½-inch slices | 5–7 minutes | 2 cups | sesame seeds |
| Corn on the cob | whole, husks removed | 4–7 minutes | 2 cups | garlic butter |
| Kale | trimmed | 5–8 minutes | 2 cups | olive oil and garlic |
| Leeks | timmed, cut in half | 5–8 minutes | 2 cups | vinaigrette |

# Steamer Setting Chart

## Vegetable Steaming Chart

| Vegetable | Size/Preparation | Cooking Time | Liquid | Seasoning Ideas Salt & Pepper Plus: |
|---|---|---|---|---|
| Okra | whole, trimmed | 6–8 minutes | 2 cups | sautéed scallions |
| Onions, pearl | whole | 8–12 minutes | 3 cups | lemon juice |
| Parsnips | peeled, ½-inch slices | 7–10 minutes | 2 cups | Italian seasoning |
| Peas, green | fresh or frozen shelled | 2–4 minutes | 2 cups | mint and lemon juice |
| Peas, sugar snap | whole pods, trimmed | 5–6 minutes | 2 cups | mint and lemon juice |
| Potatoes, all | cut into ½-inch slices | 8–12 minutes | 2 cups | parsley or dill |
| Potatoes, new | whole | 15–20 minutes | 4 cups | parsley or rosemary |
| Scallions | ½-inch slices | 3–5 minutes | 2 cups | olive oil and lemon zest |
| Spinach | whole leaves | 3–5 minutes | 2 cups | olive oil and garlic |
| Squash, butternut | peeled ½-inch cubes | 7–10 minutes | 2 cups | maple syrup |
| Turnips | ½-inch slices | 8–12 minutes | 3 cups | Italian seasoning |
| Turnip greens | coarsely chopped | 4–8 minutes | 2 cups | olive oil and garlic |
| Sweet potatoes | ½-inch chunks | 8–12 minutes | 3 cups | honey |
| Swiss chard | coarsely chopped | 3–5 minutes | 2 cups | olive oil and garlic |
| Zucchini | 1-inch slices | 5–8 minutes | 2 cups | olive oil and Italian seasoning |

# Healthy Substitutions

Use this guide to see how you can make simple ingredient substitutions that will give your recipes a healthy boost.

| Healthy Swaps | | |
|---|---|---|
| | **Instead Of** | **Substitute This** |
| DAIRY | Sour cream | Plain low-fat yogurt |
| | Milk, evaporated | Evaporated skim milk |
| | Whole milk | Fat-free milk |
| | Cheddar cheese | Low-fat Cheddar cheese |
| | Ice cream | Frozen yogurt or sorbet |
| | Cream cheese | Neufchâtel or light cream cheese |
| | Whipped cream | Light whipped topping |
| | Ricotta cheese | Low-fat ricotta cheese |
| | Cream | Fat-free half-and-half, evaporated skim milk |
| | Yogurt, fruit-flavored | Plain yogurt with fresh fruit slices |
| | Sour cream, full-fat | Fat-free or low-fat sour cream, plain fat-free or low-fat yogurt |
| PROTEIN | Bacon | Canadian bacon, turkey bacon, smoked turkey, or lean prosciutto (Italian ham) |
| | Ground beef | Extra-lean or lean ground beef, skinless chicken or turkey breast, tofu, tempeh |
| | Meat as the main ingredient | Three times as many vegetables as the meat on pizzas or in casseroles, soups, and stews |
| | Eggs | Two egg whites or ¼ cup egg substitute for each whole egg |
| OTHER | Soups, creamed | Fat-free milk-based soups, mashed potato flakes, or puréed carrots, potatoes, or tofu for thickening agents |
| | Soups, sauces, dressings, crackers, or canned meat, fish, or vegetables | Low-sodium or reduced-sodium versions |

# Healthy Substitutions

Use this guide to see how you can make simple ingredient substitutions that will give your recipes a healthy boost.

| Healthy Swaps | | |
|---|---|---|
| | **Instead Of** | **Substitute This** |
| GRAINS | Bread, white | Whole-grain bread |
| | Bread crumbs, dry | Rolled oats or crushed bran cereal |
| | Pasta, enriched (white) | Whole wheat pasta |
| | Rice, white | Brown rice, wild rice, bulgur, or pearl barley |
| FAT | Butter, margarine, shortening, or oil in baked goods | Applesauce or prune purée for half of the called-for butter, shortening, or oil; butter spreads or shortenings specially formulated for baking that don't have trans fats (Note: To avoid dense, soggy, or flat baked goods, don't substitute oil for butter or shortening. Also don't substitute diet, whipped, or tub-style margarine for regular margarine.) |
| | Butter, margarine, shortening, or oil to prevent sticking | Cooking spray or nonstick pans |
| | Mayonnaise | Reduced-calorie mayonnaise-type salad dressing or reduced-calorie, reduced-fat mayonnaise |
| | Oil-based marinades | Wine, balsamic vinegar, fruit juice, or fat-free broth |
| SUGAR | Sugar | In most baked goods you can reduce the amount of sugar by one-half; intensify sweetness by adding vanilla, nutmeg, or cinnamon. |
| | Syrup | Puréed fruit, such as applesauce, or low-calorie, sugar-free syrup |
| | Chocolate chips | Craisins |
| SAUCES | soy sauce | Sweet-and-sour sauce, hot mustard sauce, or low-sodium soy sauce |
| SALT | Salt | Herbs, spices, citrus juices (lemon, lime, orange), rice vinegar, salt-free seasoning mixes or herb blends, low-sodium soy sauce (cuts the sodium in half by equal volume while boosting flavor) |
| | Seasoning salt, such as garlic salt, celery salt, or onion salt | Herb-only seasonings, such as garlic powder, celery seed, or onion flakes, or finely chopped herbs or garlic, celery, or onions |

# Equivalents Charts

## Weight Measurements

| USA/UK | Metric |
|--------|--------|
| 1 oz. | 30 g |
| 2 oz. | 60 g |
| 3 oz. | 90 g |
| 4 oz. (1¼ lb.) | 125 g |
| 5 oz. (⅓ lb.) | 155 g |
| 6 oz. | 185 g |
| 7 oz. | 220 g |
| 8 oz. (½ lb.) | 125 g |
| 10 oz. | 315 g |
| 12 oz. (¾ lb.) | 375 g |
| 14 oz. | 440 g |
| 16 oz. | 500 g |
| 1½ lb. | 750 g |
| 2 lb. | 1 kg. |
| 3 lb. | 1½ kg |

## Length Measurements

| | |
|--------|--------|
| ⅛ in. | 3 mm |
| ¼ in. | 6 mm |
| ½ in. | 12 mm |
| 1 in. | 2.5 cm |

## Liquid Measurements

| USA | METRIC | UK |
|-----|--------|-----|
| 2 tbsp. | 30 m | 1 fl. oz. |
| ¼ cup | 60 ml | 2 fl. oz. |
| ⅓ cup | 80 ml | 3 fl. oz. |
| ½ cup | 125 ml | 4 fl. oz. |
| ⅔ cup | 160 ml | 5 fl. oz. |
| ¾ cup | 180 ml | 6 fl. oz. |
| 1 cup | 250 ml | 8 fl. oz. |
| 1½ cups | 375 ml | 12 fl. oz. |
| 2 cups | 500 ml | 16 fl. oz. |

## Abbreviations

| USA/UK | Metric |
|--------|--------|
| oz = ounce | g = gram |
| lb = pound | kg = kilogram |
| in = inch | mm = millimeter |
| ft = foot | cm = centimeter |
| tbsp = tablespoon | ml = milliliter |
| tsp = teaspoon | l = liter |
| fl oz = fluid ounce | |
| qt = quart | |

# Index

# Index

# Index

# cooking easier, healthier & better

## 150+ DELICIOUS RECIPES

New Steamer Function with Easy and Fast Steamer Recipes

2nd EDITION

**NINJA**®

**RULE THE KITCHEN**®

*4-in-1*

COOKING SYSTEM